D0455534

Air Traffic

Air Traffic

A Memoir of Ambition
and Manhood in America

GREGORY PARDLO

ALFRED A. KNOPF   NEW YORK
2018

THIS IS A BORZOI BOOK
PUBLISHED BY ALFRED A. KNOPF

www.aaknopf.com

Knopf, Borzoi Books, and the colophon are registered
trademarks of Penguin Random House LLC.

Library of Congress Cataloging-in-Publication Data
Names: Pardlo, Gregory, author.
Title: Air traffic : a memoir of ambition and manhood
in America / Gregory Pardlo.
Description: First edition. | New York : Alfred A. Knopf, 2018.
Identifiers: LCCN 2017047413 (print) | LCCN 2017060202 (ebook) |
ISBN 9781524731779 (ebook) | ISBN 9781524731762 (hardcover)
Subjects: LCSH: Pardlo, Gregory—Biography. | African American
men—Biography. | African American fathers. | Fatherhood. |
BISAC: BIOGRAPHY & AUTOBIOGRAPHY / Literary. |
BIOGRAPHY & AUTOBIOGRAPHY / Personal Memoirs. |
LITERARY COLLECTIONS / Essays.
Classification: LCC PS3616.A737 (ebook) |
LCC PS3616.A737 Z46 2018 (print) | DDC 811/.6 [B] —dc23
LC record available at https://lccn.loc.gov/2017047413

Jacket photographs courtesy of the author
Jacket design by Kelly Blair

Manufactured in the United States of America
First Edition

For Stretch

The ultimate mark of power may be its invisibility; the ultimate challenge, the exposition of its roots.

  —Michel-Rolph Trouillot, *Silencing the Past:*
  Power and the Production of History

If a New World were discovered now, would we be able to *see* it? Would we know how to rid our minds of all the images we have become accustomed to associate with the expectation of a world different from our own . . . in order to grasp the real difference that would be presented to our gaze?

  — Italo Calvino, "How New the New World Was,"
  from *Collection of Sand*

Contents

Air Traffic

An Introduction

Rt. 66

By some concoction of sugar, nicotine, prescription painkillers, rancor, and cocaine, my father, Gregory Pardlo, Sr., began killing himself after my parents separated in 2007. He measured his health and lifestyle against his will to live, and determined he had ten years left in the tank. Though he did "fuck up and live past sixty-five," as he was afraid he might, he was only a year over budget. He lived his last years like a child with a handful of tokens at an arcade near closing time. Those tokens included: access to credit, the patience and generosity of his family and friends, and any saleable assets (including, possibly, the titanium urn that contained his mother's ashes, mysteriously missing from the one-bedroom Las Vegas apartment where he chose to fizzle out). These resources had to be exhausted. He didn't want to endure penury, but neither would he ever "leave money on the table," as he often put it.

He died without leaving a will or naming beneficiaries. My brother, Robbie, and I agreed to have him cremated. No medical school would have taken him, and I didn't even entertain the idea of a casket. Robbie traveled from Willingboro, New Jersey, to Vegas to claim the body. My father had retired as a union representative for the American Train Dispatchers Association (ATDA), but without a will, my mother had to negotiate unfamiliar bureaucracies even to claim the two-thousand-dollar grievance pay the ATDA provided to cover his funeral. My father left an assortment of defaulted mort-gages, overdrawn bank accounts, and maxed-out credit cards; the remaining balance on a luxury sports car he had all but totaled; and a five-figure debt to the taxman.

He died May 12, 2016, as I was working on the final drafts of this book. Writing the book gave me an excuse to talk to him. Each time I interviewed him by phone from my house in Brooklyn, I was prepared for that to have been the last time we spoke. Yet even with all my psychic and emotional prepara-tion for his death, it was a poignant exercise to have to comb through these pages and change verb forms from present tense to past.

Robbie initially believed—sincerely, I suspect—that our father died of a broken heart. Robbie's story of our dad's death and life is very different from mine. I'm ten years older. I have a bigger file on our parents. Our mother and father were kids when they had me in 1968. They were twenty-one and nine-teen, respectively. In the heyday before 1981, before my father lost his job as an air traffic controller in the infamous strike that ended with Ronald Reagan firing thirteen thousand fed-eral employees, my parents' spirits were high. They wanted a second child—so much so that after miscarrying one who'd already entered the family imagination as "Heather," they suc-ceeded in having Robbie. Robbie was born in 1979. We were a boomtown under a single roof. The father I imprinted on was infinitely capable and resourceful and, as far as my child's-eye view could tell, had the world on a leash. Robbie knew a less idealistic, chastened version of our father, by then a man who was resigned to having been blackballed from the career that defined him. By the time Robbie outgrew the hypoallergenic cloth diapers that were delivered to our house once a month, Dad was, if only for lack of alternatives, more involved in domestic life.

The father I grew up with still resented the competing demands of an unplanned offspring. I was the mistake that he felt he was nobly taking responsibility for, and I was thus made to suffer the flexing of Big Greg's narcissism in all its demonstrative and petty renditions. I don't mean this in a self-pitying way. Whereas he wanted from me a show of gratitude, I studied him. He interpreted my scrutiny as insubordination. This made our lives adversarial. Robbie, at least symbolically, was a comfort to him. I was a threat. I was my father's rival, and he was mine. This may sound wildly self-important, but this is the prerogative—my father would agree—of the one who has outlived the other.

There is a picture of me in my mother's arms on my first birthday. Voodoo child, star child, love child. My first birthday was a Monday, *Lunes,* day of the moon. It was the day my mother turned twenty-two. Every year, the same tired joke: *Happy Birthday!* I'd grin, empty-handed and pitiful. I was the gift, the reminder of what she gave of herself, to herself, that she must tow through the cosmos in a contrapuntal orbit. I have always belonged to her, through the infinite umbilicus of fate, a Taoist Return to my origins revealed in this annual eclipse, November 24, the shared anniversary of our births. What grief, what blemished self-image did she need to bury that she would risk an accidental pregnancy with a man as superficial as my father? Yet my guilt over being the unexpected orange detour arrow of her life elevated me in importance over my father's fleeting diversions. Good and bad, I was beyond evaluation, the fulcrum of every story she might devise to tell of her life.

My parents' marriage collapsed like a shoddy circus tent on the evening we held the launch party for my first book of poems. The Creative Writers House at New York University, where I'd completed my master of fine arts degree in poetry, hosted the party. It was the fall of 2007. My father was a jealous man for his wife's attention, the success of others, and the attention of the crowd. This was the kind of crowd he coveted most: my old classmates, colleagues, and writer friends. If I'd only asked him to make a toast that night at the launch party, he might have been in better spirits. If he'd felt acknowledged, he might still be alive. That's a wild leap, I know, but thoughts like this cross my mind.

Before the party ended, he picked a fight with my mother. After he drove her two hours down the turnpike to our hometown of Willingboro, dropped her off at her father Bob's house, and told her not to come home, she discovered that he had taken her house keys from her purse. According to my mother, he wouldn't say what had provoked him or why he was upset. But I know he was throwing a tantrum over having been ignored at the book party. He was acting out. A true diva will not be upstaged.

In April 2015, days after it was announced that I'd won the Pulitzer Prize for my second book of poems, I still hadn't heard from my dad. Most of our communication was via text message, because he would get winded and need to rest after a few minutes of talking. I wanted to know if the news had reached him. He texted back, "When a Roman general conquered a town, Caesar would send a slave to ride alongside the general in the victory parade, and remind the general that he was only human."

The last time I saw him was in August 2015, at the party my mother threw at a hotel in Marlton, New Jersey, to celebrate the prize. I was surprised he made it all the way from Las Vegas to Marlton. What a wreck he had become physically; during our rare phone conversations, he complained about the multiplying failures of his body. He couldn't walk five feet without losing his breath, so he'd often sit near exits where he could get out easily to have a smoke. He'd lost half his right leg to diabetes, refusing to give up the junk foods he equated with his dignity. He was incontinent. It took a herculean effort for him to "be there" in both the emotional and physical senses, an effort you'd think was motivated by pride in his son's achievement. But I knew, as perhaps only a son can know, that I was the opening act. My father loved me, and was indeed proud of me in his complicated way, but he came to Marlton for the crowd.

He came with his motorized chair and his life-extending contraptions to give his final performance. He looked glorious, the old bull, in his matching suede jacket and pants. Determined, he ditched the chair and stood on his prosthesis, no doubt imagining himself in the mode of some hard-bitten pirate declaiming from the quarterdeck. He gave a speech that congratulated me by commemorating his own place in history, situated generationally, as he explained, between "two titans": his father and me. We were the giants standing on his shoulders.

My father didn't suffer from humility. He thought it was a deceitful affect. He favored potential over humility, and believed that showing the latter prevents indulging the former. Potential is a promissory note always worth more, not *more than,* just *more.* With humility, what you see is what you get. My druthers lie somewhere between, and this book studies that overlap. Can one aspire to Saint Augustine's humility? When I got sober and began working the steps, I got stuck on the one that says, "Made a searching and fearless moral inventory of ourselves." This book is my Step Four. That I have failed is evident in my digressions and indulgences, but the eight remaining steps are full of promise.

Part One

The Up-to-Daters Club

My mother's father, Bob, leveraged a career with the federal government to support his interests in art, science, and business, all of which he pursued quixotically, as if he'd been born into the oak and ivy security of old money. I wish I could imagine him triumphing over racial discrimination, and heeding only the command of his ambition as stories of black exceptionalism would have it. Strictly speaking, Bob was not a lone master of his fate when he left Philadelphia for the Civil Aeronautics Administration training center in Oklahoma City in 1951, the year he started out as a fledgling head of household. He was no superhero. His story is most unremarkable, especially set against the social and political backdrop of the time. Indeed, when I consider how unexceptional my grandfather was, I appreciate his unique virtues all the better.

I don't want to diminish Bob's accomplishments, but it is worth pointing out that before President Woodrow Wilson made segregation the law of the land, federal jobs supported many middle-class black families. For sure, there was plenty of discrimination in the public and private sectors, but according to "Negro Employment in the Federal Government," a

1945 article in *Phylon: The Clark Atlanta University Review of Race and Culture,* blacks held "positions such as Register of the Treasury, Assistant Postmaster General, Recorder of Deeds, and numerous positions in the consular and diplomatic services" before President Wilson's policy backlash. The article's authors report that "by 1912 there were over 19,000 jobs held by Negroes in the Federal Service." I think about the impact those jobs would have had on the lives of multiplying generations if they had been allowed to mature into pensions, home ownership, and college degrees. This may have been what Southern Democrats feared when they started demanding resignations from blacks in white-collar positions, and restricting them to "custodial and janitorial service."

Inflaming racial distrust to obscure fears of competition, the Navy Department was the first to make black employees sit behind screens so that their white colleagues would not have to see them. Under President Wilson, federal appointing officers repurposed the "rule of three" to justify not hiring qualified black applicants. According to the *Phylon* article, the rule of three "permit[ted] the appointing officer administrative discretion to select one of the three highest eligible but not necessarily the highest. . . . This rule permitted the arbitrary passing over of any Negro who stood highest on a list of eligibles." The authors concluded, "It soon came to pass that practically no Negro had a chance for appointment to a clerical position no matter how high a grade he obtained in the Civil Service examination."

When the Harvard educated businessman Monroe Trotter and other civil rights leaders called on Wilson at the White House in 1914 to ask him to help stanch the segregationist fervor, Wilson claimed he had never been spoken to so disrespectfully. He threw Trotter and his delegation out of the Oval Office and defended segregation as being in "the best interest of both races."* The "Red Summer" of 1919 saw unprecedented bloodshed and lawless attacks on black Americans aspiring to the middle class. Wilson left office in 1921.

After more than twenty years of deepening racial division, in 1941, under pressure from Eleanor Roosevelt, A. Philip Randolph, and other civil rights activists, President Franklin Delano Roosevelt established the Fair Employment Practices Committee (FEPC) to curb racial discrimination in hiring for all "war-related work" of federal agencies and contractors. The FEPC—an early iteration of affirmative action in a history of similar legislative efforts—was reviled by the segregationists, and quickly dismantled after Roosevelt's death. The committee's work, at least, made it possible for President Harry Truman to integrate the armed forces in 1948. Bob joined the federal payroll in this climate of intense racial adversity.

In 1946, the expanding Civil Aeronautics Administration Standardization Center relocated from Houston to Oklahoma City. The CAA, precursor to the Federal Aviation Administration (FAA), set up shop using leftover wartime equipment and surplus Quonset huts salvaged from the War Assets Administration. Increasingly consumer-friendly, aviation was a vital engine of commerce and postwar prosperity, and the CAA was responsible for bringing order to the unregulated industry. Oklahoma was a curious choice for the CAA because of that state's aviation history. Twenty-five years earlier in Tulsa, some three hundred people were killed in what was likely the first aerial attack on American soil.

---

* "President Resents Negro's Criticism," *New York Times,* November 13, 1914.

In 1921 Tulsa, a black teenager accused of raping a white female elevator operator in a busy hotel lobby was apprehended and jailed. Less-than-objective news of his crime spread quickly to all but ensure that the prisoner would be dragged from his cell that night, as was common practice at the time, hung from a tree, and set fire to. Empowered black residents hoped to prevent such a miscarriage of justice by guarding the jail to make sure the accused lived long enough to stand trial. The mob would not be stayed. Before long, people were shooting and screaming and running for cover.

Tulsa was rivaled in prosperity only by Oklahoma City. Its oil barons could afford, combined, a fleet of private planes, which were scrambled for service in what history would recall as the Tulsa Race Riot of 1921. These private planes were used to drop sticks of dynamite and burning balls of turpentine on the homes and businesses of black Tulsans, the wealthiest African American community in the nation. Buck Colbert Franklin, Tulsa lawyer and father of historian John Hope Franklin, described the aftermath: "the planes—now a dozen or more in number—still hummed and darted here and there with the agility of natural birds of the air."

————

In 1951, my grandfather Bob—his wife and friends called him "Shorty"—flew to Oklahoma for training as a radio technician. At the time, he lived with his wife and their toddler, my mother, in his parents' Philadelphia row house. He'd been working as a stock clerk in an electronics supply store when he took the civil service exam that qualified him for this federal training program.

It was the first time the twenty-five-year-old had traveled

beyond the Delaware Valley. When the Douglas DC-3 dragged its tail across Will Rogers Field toward the terminal in Oklahoma City, Bob and Kenneth, the two young black men from Philadelphia admitted to the program, noticed a commotion on the runway. Squeezing their faces into the oval porthole they shared, they made out pulsing cherry tops on police cruisers, and wondered aloud whether there had been an accident on the airstrip.

Bob would not have known about Oklahoma's aviation history. Even if it had been taught in schools, he hadn't seen a classroom since his father forced him to drop out in the tenth grade. Bob's father, Robert G. Parham, Sr., we called him "Rob-Pop," believed public school would not shield Bob from having to "sweep the white man's floors" for a living, and that public school would, in fact, only be an expedient for a life of such service. Bob and Rob-Pop shared a hobby as ham radio operators. The sixteen-year-old Bob picked up odd jobs at radio repair shops throughout Philadelphia. In exchange for his labor—ironically, for "sweeping the white man's floors"—Bob got to learn how electronics worked. He crisscrossed the city several times a day to get to these proto–unpaid internships.

Working in two different shops, he solicited lessons whenever possible. The skilled workmen found Bob a quick enough study that in time they relied on him to ease their workloads in addition to keeping the floors clean. Bob leveraged their reliance on him to negotiate an hourly wage. Someone mentioned that an electronics store downtown on Market Street needed a stock clerk, and he gave notice at both repair shops. He spent two years working at the store on Market Street, identifying and teasing out the functions of electronic parts throughout the stockroom until a regular customer told him about the civil service exam advertised in *The Philadelphia Inquirer.* Bob had already taught himself Morse code, a skill that helped him pass the exam.

Kenneth, unlike Bob, came from a religious home. Proud enough to avoid any racial confrontation that would reveal his second-class condition, he often reminded Bob—like a caddy with a scorecard side-mouthing prudent advice into a golfer's ear—how much liberty they were permitted in the company of white folks. Kenneth had a high school diploma, a virtual pedigree compared to Bob, and had been tutored in electrical engineering by an idealistic teacher. Bob and Kenneth couldn't have been less alike, but combined they posed a singular threat to the racial order in Oklahoma.

A crowd was gathered on the tarmac. There were pressmen and photographers filling out the crowd, which seemed to grow agitated as the plane approached. A group of policemen stood apart. Maybe there was a celebrity on the plane, Bob and Kenneth wondered. Workers rolled the gangway out to meet the aircraft. Bob and Kenneth didn't realize what the cause of the fuss was even after the sheriff approached them at the bottom of the gangway—somewhat aggressively, they felt. The sheriff's pearl-handled revolvers glinted sharply on each hip. Bob heard the shutter click of cameras as the big man announced, "I guess you know you're in the South now, boys."

Bob hadn't thought of Oklahoma as being in the South, but hearing the sheriff put it this way, he could see how that might be the case. The two men from Philadelphia were loaded into the backseat of one police vehicle while their suitcases were loaded into another. It occurred to them that *they* were the celebrities.

The mini-motorcade ferried Bob and Kenneth away from

the terminal, the crowd, and the cameras. The sheriff's deputies delivered the two men to the one rooming house in town that would accept "colored" guests: the local brothel. Here, the proprietor confirmed that Bob and Kenneth did indeed have some local renown. Their admission to the academy had been announced in the paper. They were not the first Negroes to attend the academy, but they were the first of skilled rank, and as such were rare enough to be newsworthy. In the week before classes began, however, Bob discovered he would hold that dubious honor alone. Kenneth booked a flight back to Philadelphia after he discovered that their only accommodations would be in a house of ill repute.

Bob, meanwhile, had to adjust to the brutish imperatives of segregation legible over doorways and water fountains throughout Oklahoma City, and intuit the enigmatic social codes that seemed to frame even the most mundane interactions. At first, he smiled at people, made eye contact, and said hello as if he were just any other neighbor. Disgust was not an uncommon response.

While he acclimated, he searched for more domestic accommodations, and eventually met, through the YWCA, Mr. and Mrs. Hawkins. The Hawkinses were the proprietors of a dinner club on the outskirts of the city. The Up-to-Daters Club was on the "chitlin' circuit," and because there were few venues of its kind in Oklahoma City, many popular black entertainers of the day performed there. The Hawkinses took Bob in as a boarder and let him earn extra cash waiting tables at the club on weekends. Of the numerous marquee-name entertainers to appear there, Bob would remember the young Ray Charles most fondly for having taught Bob his first blues chords on the piano.

The Up-to-Daters Club was a segregated club—meaning blacks only, as whites-only clubs were not considered segregated. But the club was popular among whites who found the atmosphere in mainstream establishments less inspiring. Bob was surprised to find the sheriff who had met him and Kenneth at the airport among the regular customers. The gregarious and foul-mouthed sheriff often entertained large tables of his deputies, their wives, and guests of the police force. Oklahoma was a dry state, so Bob had to negotiate layers of irony and contradiction as he served the white lawmen illegal spirits in this segregated nightclub. The Up-to-Daters Club in 1951 was also where Bob, as he told me, "learned to drink."

———

As the only black person on the facility, his days were marked by routine humiliation. Buses were shunned by all who could afford alternatives. And Bob, dressed like a Beat poet in black sport jacket and skinny black tie, was forced to the ass-end of these rolling asylums, prohibited from riding in the more comfortable seats at the front of the bus. Lunchtime presented medieval challenges, as there was only one mess hall, and Bob was not allowed to eat there. Neither was he allowed to bring food into any of the classrooms. A Jewish classmate, at considerable risk, smuggled food to Bob through the loading bay of the kitchen, where Bob ate his lunch each day on the wooden stairs in the shade of an awning.

The dirt road from the classroom to the mess hall led past households whose breadwinners were the caretakers and groundskeepers of the training facility and the airport at large. These families were white, and by lunchtime their children, released from school, filled the street with mischief and sport. Bob, more infamous than ever now for having dared to complete his training, forded this wind-scored path each day, trailed by kids who nettled him like deer flies, calling him nigger and kicking the red earth at his pant legs. The children's mothers looked on in amusement as they absently pinned sheets of laundry to lines in their front yards.

Bob was responsible for the maintenance and development of landing systems, systems capable of guiding aircraft in zero-visibility weather conditions. The machines he worked on communicated through radio signals that aircrafts would tune in to so precisely that they would practically carry the plane landward. After training, Bob was assigned to a municipal airport in Millville, New Jersey, where he lived with his family until my mother was eight. Bob claimed a large section of their bathroom to outfit as a radio station. My mother remembers Bob letting her announce his call sign, "W3QBP," over the airwaves.

The junior Parhams moved back to the city when Bob was promoted first to Northeast Philadelphia Airport, then to Philadelphia International. Their new home on Widener Place announced its prestige with a detached garage and its position at the end of the block of row homes. The full basement allowed Bob to build a more professional studio for his radio equipment. His enthusiasm extended to the family car, which sported a whip antenna that strained skyward like the arm of a kid with the answers to all the teacher's questions.

Perhaps feeling nostalgic for the Up-to-Daters Club, Bob outfitted the new basement with a bandstand, too. My grandmother Sarah complained that Bob was grudging with gro-

cery money while his musical inventory in the basement grew
to include a piano, a church organ, an upright bass, drums,
guitars, assorted horns, and one accordion. Bob continued to
study the piano, and soon the basement on Widener Place had
a reputation as a jazz laboratory and hangout for the black artist community.

———

Bob loved his children, but he was impatient with bourgeois
life. There was something Gaugin-like about his ambition.
Once he retired, he left his wife and family to satisfy whatever urges he had put on hold for the previous twenty years.
My grandfather died April 13, 2013, before it occurred to me
to give him the chance to determine how his story would be
interpreted, arguably more important than the story itself.
I didn't ask what drove him. He never forgave his father for
making him drop out of high school, and his relentless curiosity proved it. He'd told me that Rob-Pop had literary ambitions, and that he himself flirted with writing, too, but I didn't
know how serious either had been.

After Bob died, I found among the love letters and photographs from his various girlfriends several poems, stories, and
plays he'd written. The poems were sentimental and antiquated
in style, but the prose was socially conscious and showed the
influence of the burgeoning Black Arts Movement. The all-
night jam sessions on Widener Place had attracted writers and
actors as well as musicians. Bob befriended fellow Philadel-
phians Ed Bernard, who would later play Detective Joe Styles
on the television series *Police Woman,* and Charles Fuller, the
future Pulitzer Prize–winning playwright of *A Soldier's Play.*

Bob once answered an open call downtown to audition for the lead role in a new television series that seemed custom-made for him. He performed well enough at the audition to earn an invitation to Los Angeles for screen testing. Whether his daughters talked him out of making the trip to LA or out of pride he decided that a sitcom was beneath his artistic ambitions, Bob declined the invitation, and the role of George Jefferson in *The Jeffersons* went to rival Philadelphia actor Sherman Hemsley.

Bob landed the role of Othello at the McCarter Theatre in Princeton. Rather than commute from Philadelphia, he rented a room from George Warfield, professor of physics and engineering at Princeton University and, eventually, lifelong friend and mentor. Professor Warfield's influence drew Bob back to science and engineering, and after his run in the theater, Bob started, among other businesses, a janitorial service cleaning offices at the university. He met other members of the faculty, and soon reprised his earliest role as shop intern, picking the brains of all who would indulge his interest.

Years later, in 1989, he won a contract earmarked for minority-owned businesses, his most successful venture yet. Amtrak had sent out a request for proposals to develop computer code that would analyze data from terminals installed along train tracks. Bob's company employed his youngest daughter, Robin, and his old friends, programmers from Princeton University. Earnings from this company allowed him to buy a little neighborhood bar in Merchantville, New Jersey. The Serengeti Café & Jazz Club had a bandstand with piano, upright bass, and drums. The club was lucky to break even most months, but that was kind of the point. It brought the family together. Among his three daughters, sons-in-law, and grandkids, most of us worked at the club in some capacity at one time or another. Every Thursday night, and weekends when we couldn't afford a headline quartet, Bob played piano with the house trio, a rhythm section that welcomed musicians from across the Philadelphia area to sit in with them. For the decade that the club survived, it was legendary for jam sessions that lasted long into the night.

Student Union

Doctors tried to halt the infection at his ankle, but my father had ignored the rot for too long. He needed pruning all the way up to the knee, and lost much of his right leg to diabetes. Sitting as close to upright as he could manage in the folding bed at Our Lady of Lourdes in Camden, he dragged on an electronic cigarette, which he'd made me smuggle in for him from the Wawa on Haddon Avenue on my way to the hospital. It was strangely rejuvenating, buying cigarettes for my father again the way I had as a kid. He "lit" the thing and a tiny diode where the ember should be pulsed like a blip on a radar screen, as if to echo his weak vitals.

"You know Paddy Chayefsky," my father asked. "Wrote a movie called *The Hospital*? Well, you'd like him." He released the vapor with relish. "The way you get the nursing staff to leave you alone? Press the call button. Guaranteed at least ten minutes of undisturbed smoking if I press it." This was one of the lessons he'd taken from Chayefsky and applied to his current circumstances. He took pride in being able to project movie plots onto his life, and he believed deeply in the verity of plot contrivances sanctioned by the big screen.

All the reminders of mortality around us put me in some-thing of a clerical mood. I pried into the facts and milestones of my father's life, no longer afraid of him cutting me off or sending me out of the room. Greg Sr. got kicked out of Central High School in Philadelphia for truancy in 1965, and enrolled instead at the sprawling regional, Germantown High. He told me that was where he became president of Germantown High's first Black Student Union. I'd learned at a young age to adjust for the self-aggrandizement in my father's narratives. Problem was, so much of the way I interpret the world has come from the way *he* interprets it. I let him ramble.

My father told me that his ambitions for the Black Student Union had been in no way altruistic. He wanted to master the master's tools. Period. He wanted to show that he *could*, I guess—and he wanted to be seen doing it. He was more inter-ested in the aesthetics of protest than in the real-world impact of changing social structures. As a teenager, my father led his band of protesters to sit-ins, be-ins, drum circles, and commu-nity centers. They appeared on the public broadcast station, WHYY, he claims, and also on the neoclassical steps of school buildings. Did they constitute the voice of a community? Did they actually *represent* anyone's interests beyond their own?

The Black Student Union of Germantown High acquired a reputation for being "well-mannered" and "articulate" when, during a fateful school board meeting in the auditorium of Leeds Junior High, my father first responded to the words that became for him a rallying cry, a call to duty: *"Young man,"* someone asked, *"would you care to say a few words?"*

I imagine parents and administrators at school board meet-ings typically groaned and rolled their eyes at groups of young African American toughs, arms folded, in the aisles of auditoriums wearing black turtlenecks under dark explosive topiaries of hair. But, after word got around of the speech my father gave that night at Leeds, the young radicals from Germantown High became welcome guests at such meetings. Committees began inviting my father's group to serve as a preemptive buffer against *less* "mannered" groups of activists. Other groups would arrive at a school board meeting prepared to disrupt its proceedings only to fall silent upon recognizing my father among the white men seated behind the microphones.

———

Central High School opened in 1838. It is the nation's second-oldest continually operating public high school, and it remains among the highest-performing public schools in the state of Pennsylvania. My grandfather Samuel Pardlo, Jr., graduated from this elite institution in 1939. He expected my father to replicate the rare achievement, which, he maintained, should have been easier for my father in the 1960s, given significant advances in race relations. My father responded to this pressure with a defensive machismo ill-suited for the classroom. He feared the vulnerability and the humility that the learning process, undertaken in earnest, requires.

Once, when he was nine, my father took a walk through a park with Sam. I have a black-and-white photograph of the two of them, which I associate with this story even though, in the photograph, my father and grandfather are standing in the front yard of the family house in Willow Grove, Pennsylvania, about twenty minutes outside of Philly. In the photograph they are wearing what might be matching suits, but Sam, I know, wouldn't have gone for anything so cutesy. My dad's head is tilted at a playful angle, his mouth open as though he's in the middle of a song or telling Sam something amusing. Sam is expressionless, the disparity between their faces proving Sam's impatience. I set the still image in motion and watch as my grandfather brings his open hand up against the back of my father's head, smacking the shit out of the boy. The few times he retold this story, my father emphasized, strenuously, the lesson my grandfather was imparting: that, with life being so unpredictable, you must always be on guard. No time for idle chatter. Still, I read my dad closely for signs of what must have unfolded after the shutter clicked on the photograph, the moment the smile was wiped from his face. The lesson could not have made sense to a boy that age. My father's subsequent refusal to make himself vulnerable to authority figures rendered a classical education like the one offered at Central untenable.

The final exam for his AP philosophy class at Central helped him develop his unconscious fears into a working theory. A single directive was scrawled across the blackboard: "Explain the transcendental eye at the center of all consciousness." For forty-five minutes, he told me, he sat contemplating the silence of the blank page. By the time the period ended, he felt as bereft as he did relieved. At the order to set pencils down, he scribbled his name, the only mark on his page, humbly in the corner, before handing in this evidence of his capacity for suffering. The confounding postscript was that he received an A on the exam, confusing and demoralizing the already distrustful student. To *prepare,* my father concluded, was to cheat. Instead, he was emboldened to rely more fully on spontaneity and verbal dexterity.

"Potential" had followed my father through the halls of Central like a sullen weather system, but when he arrived at

Germantown High, my father was made to feel that he had mental abilities near clairvoyance. His depression abated. Here were the people, he decided, from whom he had been estranged, the proletariat, and among them he would shine in the right measure. He was first recruited to lead the Controversy Club, a group of students pretending toward the cultural fringe. They were an interracial collection of hippies and pot-heads who enjoyed, if the name of the club is to be taken at face value, discussing the controversial issues of the day. Through events hosted by the Controversy Club, my dad met several young black guys with whom he found he had many things in common, not the least of them being a sharp wit and a ready libido. It was through the Controversy Club, too, that he discovered his passion for smoking weed.

Out of these new friends and others, my father formed the more selective Black Student Union. In need of branding and posters, they enlisted the services of Marion Parham, a light-skinned girl as tall as my dad whom he had crushed on since childhood. Her nickname was "Stretch." Legendary as the school's best artist, Stretch had graduated from Germantown High and was in her first year at Moore College of Art. My father had civic and personal motives for enlisting Stretch to the cause—not that either he or Stretch cared to separate idealism from romance. "Dating" would not be an accurate term for their agenda-bound relationship.

One of the BSU's first offensives targeted that school board meeting at Leeds Junior High School, in the Mount Airy neighborhood. At issue was the unrest among the student body. The 1964 riot, three years earlier, on Philadelphia's Columbia Avenue, and the ones that summer in Newark and Plainfield, New Jersey, made tense what otherwise would have been dispassionate discussions around pedagogy—the achievement gap in performance between black and white students, and the adoption of a more culturally inclusive curriculum. Fear disguised itself as prudence.

Jesse, Booth, Bubby, Ridge, and "Pard," as my father was familiarly known, entered the auditorium and made themselves conspicuous. After sitting through half an hour of uninspiring political theater, my father, to play to the fear that the young men might leave and do something rash, instructed his cohort to make a show of walking out in exasperation. Whether it was my father's intended outcome or not, the chair of the meeting interrupted the discussion to set my father's future in motion: "Young man," he shouted, leaning into the microphone. "Young man! Would you care to say a few words?"

My father approached the floor mic at the foot of the stage and began. "What we have here is a failure to communicate." He cleared his throat and paused a moment, enough to allow the audience's curiosity to flirt with worry. *It only takes a cursory perusal to ascertain the disregard this august body has for the well-being of black youth. This ill will is deleterious both to these students—who make up the overwhelming majority of the student population—and the reputation of the public school system of our great and historic city. Rather than mire the conversation in resentment and suspicion, you, gentlemen, have an opportunity to demonstrate, as it was nearly two hundred years ago, that Philadelphia is the beacon of wisdom to lead the nation forward through these troubled times.* His rhetoric was further laced with lines he'd memorized from the St. Crispin's Day Speech of *Henry V,* and from the Rudyard Kipling poem "If." The point here was not merely to persuade, but to dazzle. Versions and snippets of this oration reverberated years into the future via my father's penchant for self-reference. Turgid as it was, though, his speech moved the gentlemen of the school board. He told me one audience member offered to serve as his booking agent for speaking engagements. My father declined; still, the seed was sown.

———

A coalition of students from across the city organized a strike and the ill-fated 1967 march on the Philadelphia School Board building to protest the school board's apparent refusal (through inaction) to consider requests (which had become demands) to end tracking and mandatory vocational training. These demands were presented by the citywide student coalition led by then eighteen-year-old David Richardson. Later, the 201st District of Germantown would send Richardson, at twenty-four years old—the youngest in Pennsylvania history—to serve his first of eleven terms in the Pennsylvania House of Representatives. My father and his Black Student Union played an instrumental role on the planning committee for the student strike, spending months meeting with Richardson and other activists in the basement of the Church of the Advocate, and at Rendezvous, a popular nightclub that had become Richardson's unofficial office.

I'm not sure if he told me this or if Didion is percolating, but I will speculate that my father was enamored with the prospect of being seen on television (or perhaps seeing himself) getting arrested, and that he had given a great deal of thought to the taglines he would shout at the camera as he was being shoved into a police car. But when the day of the student strike came, November 17, 1967, neither he nor Jesse, his closest friend and confidant, was in attendance. My father had reestablished his practice of ditching school, but instead of joining the march, as months of planning suggested he would, he was in bed with his new girlfriend, Stretch, and Jesse was at home with his girlfriend—facts they would both obscure by later recounting to other members of the coalition, as if they had been present, events they simply watched on the broadcast news.

Commissioner of Police Frank Rizzo, who would later be elected mayor of Philadelphia, is famously quoted as commanding the riot-geared police squad to "get their black asses," unleashing an attack on the students. Twenty-two were injured and more than fifty arrested. That passage by King Henry V forever soured my father's conscience with irony: "And gentlemen in England now abed / shall think themselves accursed they were not here, / And hold their manhoods cheap."

I'm guessing I was conceived about three months after the student march. Bob, Sarah, Sam, and Ollie: all four of my grandparents considered themselves of a social standing that did not permit being grandparents in their early forties, which made my parents pariahs to their respective families. Claiming they planned to participate in the "Solidarity Day" march, the last gasp of Martin Luther King, Jr.'s by then posthumous Poor People's Campaign, in Washington, DC, Stretch and Big Greg eloped, Freedom Riders for love, on a bus to South Carolina. He sported a gray suit his mother bought for him to wear on formal occasions. My mother, whose pregnancy was not yet showing, wore a white minidress and matching go-go boots. She was almost twenty-one, and my father was almost nineteen.

Newly wed and expecting, Big Greg was eligible for a Class 3-A exemption from the draft because of the hardship military service would pose to his wife and child. But he also would have got a Class 1-S (C) deferment, which he could claim as a college student. I like to think his decision to marry my mother resulted from more than convenience and opportunism; or that they believed, however naively, they might fulfill the promise of their lives while raising a child; or that it was an inkling of that blind commitment to pride that would be his repeated undoing over the years.

Having been offered, and accepted, a full ride at what was then Cheyney State College, the oldest historically black college in the nation, my father improvised an income through speaking engagements, lectures, tutoring, and mentoring programs ("I taught black kids how not to scare white folks," he once told me). This supported him and his young family until the demands of his ambition outstripped the limits being a student placed on that ambition, and he resolved to drop out of college in order to pursue his activism full-time, prophetically casting his eyes skyward like the fashionable pose modeled in images of populist revolutionaries.

My maternal grandfather, Bob Parham, who began his career as a technician for the Federal Aviation Administration, was held in such esteem by the early seventies that he was allowed to spearhead an initiative to recruit and prepare minorities and women for careers in air traffic control. Bob traveled across the country, but he was based at Philadelphia International Airport, in the city his ancestors had called home for five generations. Bob taught recruits, preparing them for the civil service exam, the first hurdle toward qualifying for training at the FAA Academy in Oklahoma City. For years, the exam had proved inscrutable to nearly all but white men with either a college education or closely comparable military experience. In the political environment of the day, however, a glaring lack of diversity among public employees was a liability for federal institutions, legally as well as morally. The Equal Employment Opportunity program that Bob oversaw supported recruits like my dad. Bob's distaste for the young man who'd led his daughter astray was now outweighed by the need to provide for a grandson, and he invited my father to participate in the EEO program, although Big Greg was too proud to accept his father-in-law's help unconditionally.

"He almost got me fired!" Bob said, recalling the havoc caused by my father's performance on the civil service aptitude test for air traffic control. The matter came to his supervisors' attention because my father scored suspiciously high on the exam. Someone therefore accused Bob not only of preparing my father for the test according to the program's mandate, but also of feeding him the answers.

In fact, however, both men confirmed that my dad had refused Bob's preparatory course altogether. Yes, he'd accepted Bob's invitation to shepherd him through the formalities, but my father refused to "grant that kind of access," he told me, to his new father-in-law. He would not let Bob see him in the vulnerable state of apprenticeship. Beyond that, my father wanted to prove how useless, how far beneath him, was Bob's condescending notion of tutelage.

In my father's version of the story, he did so well on the original written exam that not only did he prove himself beyond the need for any help from Bob, but the FAA brass, incredulous, refused to accept his score was possible. They demanded he sit for an oral exam with FAA officials, to see for themselves the young man who claimed to have had no left-handed support.

Loser

I mplicitly, I learned from my father that there was no glory in just *winning*. Capricious, pendular, my father's wont was to sway by the rope of his devotions, to and fro, and winning was a one-way trip. What point was there in winning if it precluded the possibility of a comeback? Winners win. So what. The story stinks of empire.

He was a passionate man, my father. He claimed to have been so sensitive as a child that he wept when Mr. Whipple squeezed the Charmin. Thus, gridiron dramas would bear for him the gravitas of Agincourt.

"Give the ball to the retarded boy," my father would growl in the voice of his weepy inner storefront preacher. "Give it to the gimp!" And he'd pump his fist, as if snatching a fly from the air, to punctuate the rhetorical flourish. This was his shorthand for the archetypal comeback story, and he told it so often—he had tapped it with tuning forks, held it up against the light, refined the story to one cry for the hero to rise from a life of relentless defeat.

My father's world operated on homespun destiny, the kind of destiny that was dictated by character and the inevitability of Hollywood endings. I'm talking about the power you have to shape the story. The power to recognize the decisive moment when that moment is presented to you.

When we give the ball to the "retarded boy," as my father's ironic affection would have it, against all good sense, when all seems lost, we believe that the one with the most odds to overcome is the one who is most prepared to produce a miracle. The individual who has labored under the greatest weight of doubt is most poised to subvert the more common order. It is the mundanity of human evolution condensed to an observable, measurable fact. It is evidence of God or the thrill of the high-stakes gamble. For we are expressing our conviction that somewhere, at some point, somebody told the gimp to love himself, and that love will win out.

I'd suck my teeth when my father got into one of his praise-the-underdog moods. It was a state of reverie he slipped into, leaving me to wait for him in the lobby of his imagination. I might have been inclined to enjoy it, too, if it held out even an implied invitation to join him. In my solitude, I dreamed of being the hero my father cheered for. Cue filmic dissolve. Cue dream sequence:

Early autumn, the first smell of woodsmoke from chimneys, a yet-too-early wool sweater scratching the neck, sweating the skin under the crisp backpack that still holds the silica gel packet that came with it. On my way home a deliquescent sun lamps the pine-dipped breeze, needles underfoot like uncooked pasta. It's the end of the school day and I hear the bass drum overlaid with a ratcheting snare. The snarl of horns is like a traffic jam in the distance until it finds its rhythm and, oh shit, *I recognize the tune is Kool & the Gang's "Celebration" or Steve Miller Band's "Fly Like an Eagle." I sprawl like a hobo under a linden on someone's lawn where the mower has made lush diagonal stripes, and enter a daydream where my arms stretch out for the ball that is ricocheting off of someone else's helmet for a change and into my hesitant possession, giving me the one immaculate chance I've been rehearsing in my mind for years: to carry the music of everyone around me, carry that tide of conviction riding on me for once because my dad is the coach and he has opened the window of providence and before anyone can stop me I'm gone and for now, I'm safe; the other team can't find me although I am weaving around them, cloaked in the confidence of my tribe. All any of them would have to do is hold out an arm and I'd be clotheslined flat, but no one does. It doesn't occur to them that I don't know what I'm doing, that I'm running on the residual fumes of my peers' self-esteem. I triumph because no one who wants to stop me is aware how easily they can.*

———

In second grade I started exhibiting behavioral problems. We had moved to Farragut Court, in Fairmount Park, one of the two subdivisions of row houses in Willingboro, and I was attending the nearby J. Creswell Stuart Elementary School. Between sleep and work and school, my father, who worked rotating shifts as an air traffic controller, and I crossed paths rarely and at random. By second grade I was getting distracted from schoolwork easily. My mother tried creative solutions. Behavior modification. Classical conditioning. I had a collection of flat rocks I'd found in the creek that ran behind Fairmount. She picked one of them the size of a cassette tape, and painted it yellow. We named it "the Good Rock." It went to school with me. If I behaved myself in school all day, the teacher would send me home with the Good Rock. Otherwise no Rock, and I came home alone. The Days of Rock were met with positive reinforcement. On the Days of No Rock I faced consequences.

My father devised punishments that were cunning and proud. He dropped the family dictionary like a Christmas ham on my rickety desk and gave me, with nothing more to go on than the mere attire of its pronunciation, an unfamiliar word. "Disconsolate," for example. He would enunciate the word with the monotone of a spelling bee announcer. I had to find the definition of the word and then find, in that definition, another word I did not understand. I was then to look up that subsequent word and so on until I could prove to my father's satisfaction that I understood every word in the definition clearly, verifying the lexical descent from my original word, at which point he might or might not assign me a new word. The ordeal couldn't have lasted more than half an hour each time, but as I remember it I spent entire evenings at my desk heaving pages the size of car mats. As a result of this experience, for years to come, indeed, in *perpetuity,* my father's vocabulary words continue to occur to me with a hint of irony, announcing their status in italics.

It may have added to my frustrations that second grade was the year I was diagnosed as both asthmatic and "hyperactive." Our doctor recommended the Feingold Diet. My mother eliminated from my diet *all* foods containing artificial flavors, colors, and preservatives. One day I was swilling half pints of chocolate milk with my Skippy peanut butter sandwiches with grape jelly that tasted more like purple Jell-O for lunch. The next day I was rationed skim milk with sunflower seed butter and spreadable fruit sandwiches while my classmates gargled the silky goodness of brown cows.

I learned to distinguish the bad stuff on every food product's label. Scanning the list of ingredients was like playing slots. The ingredients present in the largest amounts are listed first and in descending order, so I checked off each ingredient with mounting excitement only to be dejected, each time, by finding there, at the end, artificial flavors and colors. I started going straight to the end after realizing the vast majority of packaged foods contain, if not artificial flavors and colors, then, like getting seven, seven, cherry: "preservatives." I was a Cub Scout, and valued my integrity above all else. I never cheated. It didn't even cross my mind to sneak a snack cake or taffy a classmate offered me. Once, when a friend offered a piece of bubble gum, I asked him to hold it for me in his desk while I checked with my mother. The next day I came in with the verdict: no, and I had to watch as he cheeked the Hubba Bubba reeking of that scent I would forever know covetously as purple.

Virginia Santiago was part of the reason I started to improve in school. To get her attention I made myself a sympathetic victim of circumstance. I'm sure that, even then, I recognized that Virginia fit the mold of a girl whose looks my father would approve of. I didn't know where Puerto Rico was or anything about its ambiguous racial history. But Virginia's loopy afro puffs were pulled tight across her head in sections combed smooth as a vinyl record. Her complexion and her full lips suggested she was someone who should be cast in the role, opposite me, of the love interest. At recess, I engineered conflicts that ended with the class bully punching me in the stomach. She responded to my self-inflicted injuries with care and attention.

A passionate child, I practiced abject submission to beauty: like an amorous opossum, I was docile, ready to be struck senseless with want. "Passion" is a word derived from the Latin for "suffer." The Feingold Diet may have calmed my hyperactivity. But the fact that I was disciplined enough to refrain from eating so much as a marshmallow in the first place, that I could master self-denial and delayed gratification, was owing to my appetite for suffering.

———

The way he would tell it, years later, my mother left *him*. My father had called me, presumably so I would rally to his defense and approve his indignation, but I gave him no quarter. Instead I gave unwelcome advice. "Embrace it," I said. I told him to get himself a gym membership and to start dating. I listed other possibilities: travel, start collecting something, become a ship's captain, go back to school. I knew I pinched a nerve, but I couldn't help myself.

He gaveled the conversation to a close. "I'm not you," he said.

He was unwilling to reinvent himself, which felt too much like cheating. Change happened *out there*. Nothing less than a miracle would rescue him now.

What Is Your Quest?

My father's questions were abrupt and random. Bridge Keepers, I called them, after the scene in *Monty Python and the Holy Grail*. I was arrested at the cliff side. Across the fog-veiled Gorge of Eternal Peril stood my father's love. *What is the airspeed velocity of an unladen swallow?*, he'd ask. My father's game was cruel. His oppressive shadow gave my life purpose and meaning.

"A first-rate intelligence," my father would say, "is one on which nothing is lost." And this: "Learning is just a kind of remembering."

At best, he felt teachers were glorified grief counselors assigned to help unfortunate kids cope with their stupidity. At worst, in the great soup kitchens of public education, teachers were there to ladle out the slop. His job as a parent was to create the conditions under which my innate (read: inherited) intelligence could find expression. He dowsed the fields of my psyche to vent what atavistic deposits might be trapped beneath the strata of generations. *What's an eight-letter word for a high-temperature melting pot?*, he might ask over the white noise of our radial tires on the pavement, which I would have mistaken for a lullaby. My need for his approval would form the crucible out of which I still struggle to climb.

He pointed to an old photograph as evidence of my early exposure to science. It is a picture of me sitting in a periwinkle pedal car, the color echoed by the light of the television behind me. My pajama feet poke out below the steel side panels, while Neil and Buzz on the TV, awash in starshine, totter on the chalky particulate of the moon like paper cutout children. Why I failed to harness such a moment—the kind that might carry a kid toward a career in astrophysics, say—is the subject of sad speculation.

My parents were giddy about our prospects at the start of our lives together, as if each morning found us all chugging up the chain lift of a Six Flags coaster. Their confidence gave the future a foreshortened aspect, enticing them to thrill at the idea of the next ride and the next. It was madness, living in a certain future that was fixed on the visible horizon. My father called it our "potential," a kind of untested, and thus unquestionable, exceptionalism.

My mother signed Robbie and me up for piano lessons, tennis club membership, comparatively good schools. For third and most of fourth grades, I became a carpetbagger traversing parks to attend a public school better than the one authorized by our address. Each "park," as the subdivisions in my Levitt-built hometown were called, had its own elementary school where most children arrived by bike or foot. It was conspicuous when my mother and I lumbered to the curb in front of Country Club Ridge Elementary each morning in our gravel-throated '74 Corvette. The inevitable comments and universal (as far as I knew) admiration for our family car from schoolmates and teachers confirmed this distinguished me among the tow- and tousle-headed scions of Country Club Park. I name-dropped the Corvette frequently as a reminder that, even with all of their orthodontic headgear and their pranks brought home from summer camps, I belonged among them.

Midway through fourth grade we did move up to a better neighborhood. Perry lived across the street. He was in fourth grade, too, but I was finishing out the year at Country Club Ridge while Perry attended Twin Hills Elementary. Perry was into model airplanes and slot cars. Throttling the control, I whipped the inferior car Perry loaned me off the track at every turn. I pretended to share his enthusiasm while at home I penciled designs of Aston Martins and concept cars I invented or copied from pictures in magazines. There was plenty to qualify us as soul brothers, beyond the coincidence that he was the only other black kid on our street at the time.

One afternoon my father offered to take me and Perry to the hobby shop in Country Club Plaza. Perry had allowance money he'd saved for a new slot car, and I hoped without asking that my father might give me money for a slot car, too, since I'd never owned one. Perry and I scrambled into the backseat of my father's Chrysler New Yorker, a car he bought to match the Corvette: silver with a burgundy leather interior. The car had whitewall tires and wire wheels. New at the time, it boasted what the dealership called a "moon roof." Because the New Yorker was my father's private sanctuary—not a family car—this trip to the hobby shop had an air of homosocial induction. From the backseat, behind my dad, I could see his eyes in the rearview. Perry was showing off a new calculator watch. I showed Perry how to spell "hell" by turning his wrist around after typing the numbers 1-1-3-4. My dad used his TV announcer voice. "What's the oldest, largest timepiece in the world?"

"What?" I said. One of my father's rules: if you have to ask for a question to be repeated, you sure enough don't know the answer.

Then, silence as Perry approached the stage to accept the trophy. "Big Ben," he intoned into some microphone streaked with feedback and echo, hushing the masses assembled in the imaginary stadium conjured by his triumph. I thought my dad was leaning forward to wink at me in the mirror, but instead he grimaced slightly and pinched an ingrown hair on his cheek.

I'd fumbled his Bridge Keepers before, and when I did so he bared his teeth and made the sound of a buzzer to indicate I'd answered incorrectly or that my time had run out and offer as consolation prizes trips to textile factories in Central America or diamond mines in Angola. Never before, though, had one of my blunders been so clearly contextualized by the competence of a peer. No consolation prize this time. My father started the car, hooked his elbow around the passenger-side headrest, and backed out of the driveway.

Air Traffic

Monday, August 3, 1981

Around two-thirty in the afternoon the eggs land wide of us along the highway. A group of air traffic controllers, their wives, and kids, we carry signs emblazoned with the logo of PATCO, the Professional Air Traffic Controllers Organization, and chant a medley of protest slogans most of us are learning for the first time. "United," we cry, "we will never be defeated." I'm the one with the Phillies cap and the sky blue Keds, Little Greg, walking the picket line beside his father. We are the only two black people in the group. Notice the downward cast of my eyes as my father bellows at the frothing traffic in response to the hecklers strafing us from passing vehicles.

"I take it you're not in this for the sport!" he shouts. And when he throws his hands up and cries, "What, and leave show business?" he brandishes his placard like a spear.

"Figure it out," he tells me when he mistakes the look on my face for confusion. Of everyone here, I'm the one who has the least trouble deciphering his private meanings. As the world's leading scholar on Gregory Pardlo, Sr., I know these pronouncements he's polished, these homemade koans impenetrable to reason, that were once the punch lines of tired jokes. The jokes themselves are vestigial. He no longer needs them, confident his enemies will notice the deft lacerations of his wit in some later moment of quiet reflection. Uncharacteristically reckless now, he heaves them without accuracy nor discrimination at the passing traffic.

Highway grit settles across my brow and our picket line warps in the heat. Although many cars honk in solidarity with the air traffic controllers' strike, odds are the honk will precede a driver's flipping us the bird. Or worse. Nothing, though, causes me to question the righteousness of our mission. In this, at least, I hold my father infallible.

He glistens, vaguely overweight. His beard and afro round out his chubby face. Sun catches in the penumbra of his hair when he turns to face me and I squint until I fit into his shadow. The stretch marks beneath his sweat-stained shirtsleeve scribble a polygraph on the trunk of his bicep. How long had the union been preparing for this? It's been the center of concern in our house for weeks. When I woke up this morning my mother confirmed the word was out: strike! Seven thousand flights across the United States were canceled.

We tramp the gravel, level the asters and sedge grass on the roadside. There is garbage; there are wildflowers. Convection blurs our view of the terminals hulking off in the distance. Newark. In the week leading up to the strike, before negotiations failed to produce an acceptable contract for the union, a Los Angeles–area controller named Gerald W. McCormick published an op-ed in the *L.A. Times*. Writing with the patronizing tone of a high school disciplinarian, he listed several occupations that were better paid than controllers. "I'm not suggesting these [other] jobs don't have value," he assured readers. "What I'm asking is this: Are your cars, toilets and entertainment more important than your safe passage from A to B on an airliner?" In the context of the impending strike, the question was less rhetorical than it was threatening.

This is the first day we actually form a picket line, and already I'm impatient for it to be over. I can smell my father's uncertainty. I can't ask him the real question. I can't ask him, because he doesn't know—an ignorance neither of us cares to admit—when he can go back to work and when we can return to our once triumphant lives.

———

If the purpose of a picket line is to obstruct passage in and out of the offending place of business, then our presence along Routes 1 and 9, skirting the airport, was entirely symbolic. We obstructed nothing. Another objective of the picket line, though, is to shame the agents of power with the picketer's conspicuous discontent, and, through that display, to gain public sympathy and support. Our picket line hoped to "demonstrate" that we were there at the workplace, without deceit, simply refusing to work. We wanted to be *seen* withholding labor; otherwise we could have been somewhere riding go-carts and eating soft ice cream. But there was no office window through which our chants might annoy an executive or foreman as he curled his lip and glared down at us through the slats of blinds he parted with two anxious fingers. There was no public to engage with pamphlets and handshakes and signatures on petitions. We were on the side of a highway, for chrissakes. We didn't have petitions anyway.

———

Earlier that day, Monday, August 3, 1981, President Reagan had issued an ultimatum, appearing at a press conference in the Rose Garden at the White House, wearing a gray suit and a red-and-blue candy-striped tie, his hair pomped back like some superannuated R&B singer. Each controller had taken an oath, he remarked, swearing not to participate in any strike against the government, and so, pursuant to an oft-flouted statute in Title 5 of the United States Code banning federal employees from striking, air traffic controllers were "in violation of the law." Then, with that preternatural calm of his, which looked so much like goodwill, he laid it out: "If they do not report for work within forty-eight hours, they have forfeited their jobs and will be terminated."

It had been the biggest joke in the days leading up to the strike. Whenever anyone in the union hall voiced a concern or fear about the outcome of the strike, the reply, met with laughter, was the same: "What are they going to do, fire us all?" It was more than arrogance. Less than a year earlier, in return for a carefully worded letter from a politician on the campaign trail, PATCO, headed by Bob Poli, had endorsed Reagan's bid to oust the incumbent President Carter.

October 20, 1980

Dear Mr. Poli:

I have been briefed by members of my staff as to the deplorable state of our nation's air traffic control system. They have told me that too few people working unreasonable hours with obsolete equipment has placed the nation's air travelers in unwarranted danger. In an area so clearly related to public safety the Carter administration has failed to act responsibly.

You can rest assured that if I am elected President, I will take whatever steps are necessary to provide our air traffic controllers with the most modern equipment available and to adjust staff levels and work days so that they are commensurate with achieving a maximum degree of public safety . . .

I pledge to you that my administration will work very closely with you to bring about a spirit of cooperation between the President and the air traffic controllers.

Sincerely,
Ronald Reagan

———

Now, by threatening to fire and replace striking workers, not only had President Reagan ended the gentleman's agreement to overlook the Taft-Hartley rule forbidding federal employees from striking, an agreement that had endured a postal workers' strike in 1970 and earlier work slowdowns from PATCO itself, but he had also legitimized termination as a response to labor disputes, dealing a critical blow to labor worldwide.

After the president read his prepared statement, he was joined at the lectern by Secretary of Transportation Drew Lewis, someone for whom the controllers seemed to reserve a special hatred because of his "bad cop" attitude, and Attorney General William French Smith, who informed the media that they intended "to initiate criminal proceedings against those who have violated the law." Key figures in the strike would be arrested and jailed. "How soon would these criminal proceedings be initiated?" one of the journalists among the press corps asked. "Probably by noon today" was the answer.

Officially, my father was president of the Newark tower branch, or "local," of PATCO. Given his charisma and penchant for theatrics, he was often asked to speak to the press. By default, he became a very public face in the Northeast region. His would be a high-profile arrest. At home, watching the evening news, it was easy for me to picture my dad, heroically defiant, in handcuffs and leg irons, being led across the screen. The image turned fearsome when I thought about what would happen to him after I turned off the television.

In reality, I had little reason to fear. My father would never suffer the indignity of a jail cell. That night, he went on the lam, and I didn't see him for a week. When he did return home, he was careful not to park on our street in case the marshals drove by looking for him. In the days following the strike, the Justice Department arrested a handful of union officials, and issued indictments for dozens more. My father escaped legal prosecution, but suffered in other, lasting ways.

My mother and I had stayed in Philadelphia when, in 1971, my father left to attend the FAA Academy in Oklahoma City. Conveniently, his first assignment was home at Northeast Philadelphia Airport. My mother and I visited the tower often, as families were allowed to do back then. I would pass the time surveying the runways through binoculars. My parents soon bought their first house, a four-bedroom Cape Cod in Willingboro, New Jersey, within commuting distance of Philadelphia. The move was overly ambitious and, within a year, they discovered they could not afford the mortgage on the house. We moved to my paternal great-grandfather Sam Sr.'s house, recently vacated by his passing, in Willow Grove, Pennsylvania. In that one rent-free year, my parents saved enough to buy another, more modest house in Willingboro, in a subdivision of row houses. Our neighbors were mostly young professionals at the start of their careers.

My parents threw parties. They attended parties. My father was at ease among new friends and acquaintances until someone made what he might consider to be an intellectual comment. Then he turned competitive. Standing among some of the other dads at a cookout once, my father got caught up in what he described as one neighbor's insufferable self-importance. "Do you remember him," my father asked me. "He was such a dickhead. Took every opportunity to remind us he was getting a PhD at Temple."

It seems the guy had noticed a plane overhead, and wondered with a sigh, "Just imagine what country, what remote part of the world they must be off to."

"They're not going," my father said. "They're coming. He's on approach to runway twenty-two left at Philly International." Responding to the question this man had failed to ask, my father conceded, "That's what *I* do."

When he was promoted from Northeast Philly to Newark International Airport, the news confirmed a narrative of progress that we had already taken for granted. Rather than move closer to Newark, my parents moved us to yet another house in Willingboro. My father's commute to work was an hour and a half in each direction, but he would have it no other way. With three bedrooms and an in-ground swimming pool, this new house, in Twin Hills, one of the tonier developments, meant the Pardlos had arrived. It was 1976. I was eight years old; my father was twenty-seven.

————

Aside from collecting unemployment checks, controlling air traffic is one of the most stressful occupations a family can rely upon. The job required an extraordinary attention span and presence of mind; the consequences for a mistake are fatal and existential. Think of Horton carrying all of Whoville on the head of a clover. Gerald McCormick described the conditions in his 1981 op-ed, explaining that a controller's daily operations are "spelled out in an inch-thick [FAA] manual of regulations that must be committed thoroughly to memory." He continued:

> There's no time to refer to it when several aircraft are passing into, out of and through the controller's assigned airspace, sometimes at the rate of five or six per minute. The controller must simultaneously give the correct instructions to each and log its call sign, type, altitude, route, destination, time and other data on a small strip of paper. This log becomes a legal document, so it must be perfect. At the same time, the controller must answer and make calls on up to 40 phone lines and keep the one or two (usually one) assisting controllers informed about each move.

Bring that controller—whose workday consists of giving instructions he hopes will not cause any of the green dots on the radar screen to disappear, instructions he hopes will not be met with screams from the cockpit transmissions in his ears—bring that controller home each day, and see how easily he adjusts to the tenderness of domesticity. My father maintained a regimen of isolation and self-medication that allowed him to cope with the constant pressure, only instead of a martini after work in a favorite chair, my father smoked a joint in his bedroom. Or two. Reagan would not establish mandatory drug testing until 1986. Evenings and "weekends" (which was whenever he had a day or two off of work, rarely consecutively), my father smoked modestly, and he kept, on his nightstand for many years before and after the strike, a quarter ounce of weed, rolling papers, roach clips, and a marble pipe, all on a bamboo serving tray he'd got in a tourist shop in the Bahamas.

The 1981 strike was called to leverage demands that included improved working conditions, a reduced workweek, and the replacement of outmoded equipment. According to Bob Poli, the PATCO president, 89 percent of the workforce never made it to retirement because of stress. The reduced hours, it was hoped, would address safety concerns around controller fatigue. And another thing: the controllers and their families wanted earlier retirement for those few who actually made it that far, as well as an increase in pay.

Perhaps unwisely, the union voiced a number of ancillary demands, like free "FAM," or familiarization flights— accommodations in the jump seat of commercial cockpits— which could be rationalized as necessary for controllers to get familiar with the pilots' experience and the environment actually shaped by controllers' instructions. The White House cast demands like these as unnecessary perks, and the public sympathized with Reagan, the chagrined Gipper (or, as Gore

Vidal called him, "our acting president"). PATCO's strike soon became a fiasco of diminishing morale and failed public relations.

———

The National Labor Relations Board (NLRB) is an independent government agency charged with enforcing the 1935 National Labor Relations Act. This act protects employees from being fired as a result of union activities. The 1938 Supreme Court decision in *NLRB v. Mackay Radio,* however, empowered employers to recruit strikebreakers, or "scabs," to permanently replace striking workers. The Supreme Court determined that striking workers remained employees throughout the duration of the strike, but that employers were under no obligation to later discharge workers hired to replace those striking employees. Employees could strike without fear of being fired, but there was no guarantee their positions would still exist when the strike ended. Because of the Mackay doctrine, workers in the United States are dependent upon employers' willingness to bargain in good faith.

Mackay, a legal foundation for countering organized labor, may have seemed redundant. It is illegal to manipulate the abstract financial instruments, like currency, stocks, and bonds, that represent the value of labor, but it is not illegal to manipulate labor itself. In 1938, corporate executives had devised and widely adopted the "Mohawk Valley formula," a strategic plan to quell strikes. In response to a 1936–37 strike against Remington Rand, a typewriter manufacturer, the Mohawk Valley formula, so-named for the location of the New York State plant, offered a means of influencing public perception by accusing strikers of being un-American, and depicting strike organizers as radicals, agitators, and carpetbaggers. This plan was initially intended for use *in the event* of a strike, but its preference for intimidation and manipulation over the costlier and more common hiring of violent strikebreakers (thugs, known criminals, so-called special policemen, Pinkerton private security agents, and, not infrequently, the police force itself) sustained a culture of fear and obedience among the workforce. In this culture, workers would come to view collective bargaining, however advantageous to them, as an obstruction of their "right to work." They might even view each other as competitors and threats.

Strikebreaking had become formalized by 1981. President Reagan had only to apply strategies proved through generations of what by then had become a sophisticated science. Reagan had the law in his one hand and federal agents to enforce it in the other. It hardly mattered that the controllers had no viable alternative domestic market for their specialized skills.

PATCO nonetheless believed the strike could be successful if it achieved and maintained 100 percent participation of its members. If there were no scabs, the union believed that the government would see its members were irreplaceable. Surely, it was absurd to think the FAA could replace thirteen thousand specially trained controllers. And by demonstrating they had a monopoly on their skill set, PATCO leadership further believed they could counter the government's monopoly on control towers. It was a gamble, and they were betting against the house.

PATCO believed the strike was an unfortunate escalation of negotiations toward a long-term agreement with their bosses, the federal government. The controllers hoped their actions, debilitating air traffic worldwide at an expense of millions per day, would cause President Reagan to meet their demands, pacify them quickly, and invite them kindly back to work. They'd hoped the strike would pass like a brief tantrum. After the strike began, they would have accepted even token concessions to get them back to the bargaining table. Nonetheless, they were prepared to go "the distance" even though no one knew what that meant.

President Reagan, eight months into his first term in office, treated the strike as a challenge to his authority. By his deadline, August 5, only twelve hundred striking controllers had returned to their posts. The president made good on his threat. He fired the truant 11,345 controllers, and banned them from federal employment for life. (Bill Clinton lifted the ban in 1993.)

Armed with several contingency plans, the moment the strike was called, the president replaced striking controllers with a skeleton crew of military personnel, FAA brass, new hires ushered through training, and, of course, controllers who had chosen not to strike: scabs. Rumors abounded that the skies were plagued with near-misses and flights rerouted to alternate airports, but no deaths were ever reported. (It was ruled that the crash of Air Florida Flight 90 into the frozen Potomac on January 13, 1982, which killed seventy-eight, was due to errors by the pilot and crew.) The public suffered an inconvenience on the magnitude of a gas shortage or a natural disaster, and for that inconvenience, by and large, the public blamed PATCO. Although diehards continued to picket for weeks, the strike officially ended in its third day, the fifth of August, 1981, the day striking controllers were terminated. The Reagan administration won an order decertifying PATCO altogether on October 22, 1981, and rewarded scabs for their loyalty. Several of these rewards—upgraded equipment, regularized work schedules, and reduced hours—met PATCO's original demands.

———

Men like my father, many of whom may have been disinclined to pursue a college education, took on average three years to reach basic competence in the tower and five to qualify as journeyman, but few even make it out of the gate. Those able to hurdle the initial civil service exam faced a 50 percent washout rate at the academy. Those who did complete the five months of intensive training at the academy in Oklahoma City had to then qualify on each of the positions in the tower, each one with its own specific area of responsibility, such as ground control or approaching aircraft.

When I asked my father what it felt like to direct air traffic, he said to *think of it as an upside-down wedding cake,* trying to depict for me the cone of sky the control tower is responsible for. *A colossal cake, upside down. Each layer larger with rising elevation.*

I get it, I said, and I thought I did. But "Continental Flight 145, a Boeing 737," seemed to me indistinguishable from "Pan Am Flight 867, an L-1011." "How do you keep all that shit in your head?" I asked. For my sake, he tried to explain things as simply as possible.

Think of each plane as an "idea" that pops into your head, he said. *They're all important ideas but some aren't as pressing as others. Regardless, you have to keep them all in mind. You can have more than a dozen ideas in mind at one time and you have to make sure they stay distinct. Let's say Teddy Pendergrass might be one idea, for example. Or funnel cake;*

aluminum siding; potholes; the Dagobah system; Bimini. That would only be six aircrafts. We're keeping it real simple. Somehow you have to keep them all located in your mind while you're handing some off, exchanging their information with the other controllers. All your delicate ideas have to remain perfectly clear and distinct in your mind at all times.

In other words, my father's job prohibited him from synthesizing information—the process by which knowledge is formed, the process by which we *know* something. He was prohibited, in essence, from learning; he was mechanized, an arrow in the quiver, a rod in the fasces, restricted to a bureaucratic engagement with data.

You can't mix up anyone else's ideas with your own. Everyone in the tower keeps a regular pattern of thought inside the wedding cake, so you have to know those patterns in addition to your own. With your coworkers it's like having an unending argument with multiple wives; you have to be able to read everyone's mind, and predict their next thoughts, but you have to do it without getting distracted by real or imagined embellishments.

What makes it tricky, my father said, *is that some of your ideas—you can sense them, but they haven't really occurred to you yet. You don't yet have words for them. These make up the rhythm of arrivals and departures that you know will occupy the major routes at routine intervals. They're just a feeling pricking your ears. Each idea is unique—some are slow to reach you and sink like jellyfish while others swoop in like flying squirrels—but they all fit into the same physical grammar. More than anything else, the one rule that matters is spacing. The one true element of the universe: emptiness, incremental*

negations, putting nothings between somethings—that's what
makes order of the chaos.

No plane can arrive or depart of its own volition because
controllers determine the movement of every aircraft on the
ground and in the air. Granted, some planes need to make
an emergency landing (bird strike, mechanical failure, etc.),
and jump into the mix unexpectedly. And then some planes
just need to pass through the airspace without landing. Each
airline is a small nation unto itself, with its own schedules
and rhythms, but at the end of the day, the control tower dic-
tates who comes and goes, and when. This makes a skyful of
pilots like an orchestra of musicians from wildly varying cultural backgrounds. They have to be made to play in harmony
and in rhythm, but can't ever be allowed to hear each other's
instruments.

At Newark International, my father, among a crew of five,
could be in radio contact with eighteen to twenty flights an
hour, weaving them through airspace stocked, like a giant koi
pond, with 750 to 1,000 aircraft. Like some byzantine highway
interchange in the sky—the kind of thing you see outside Dal-
las, for example. And if the orchestration were ever to falter? A
traffic jam, or worse. When the planes are made to circle they
are said to be "stacked." Needless to say, this makes everybody
nervous.

In addition, each plane, from the turboprop regional jet to
the 747, behaves differently in the wind. And the wind itself:
tracking wind speeds associated with an advancing air mass
is but a small part of the general meteorological chops everyone in the tower must have. The Newark tower must keep
up-to-the-minute tabs on traffic and weather conditions at

JFK and LaGuardia as well. But global weather patterns are the ultimate concern.

What do I miss about the tower? The weather, he said. *I miss watching it rain on half the airport.* He described watching a rain cloud float in and burst like a confetti cannon above the hangars to the east while the sun sparked like an elevated train over the western parking lot, bejeweling car windshields. Such was the view from Olympus.

———

In *Collision Course: Ronald Reagan, the Air Traffic Controllers, and the Strike That Changed America,* Joseph A. McCartin explains that, during training, controllers were "taught to speak in a quick, clear, calm, and confident manner in the most stressful situations so they never distracted or concerned the pilots with whom they communicated, no matter how harried or worried they felt."

At home, though, my dad's language was often dismissive, hostile, and unpredictable. He was fond of saying "children should be seen and not heard," but there were indications that he could barely tolerate the sight of children. A puzzlingly complex command like "Go tell your mother she wants you," intended to stun you into perplexity, meant he wanted you gone. More slapstick directives, however, might have indicated only that he found your presence annoying. "Go play in traffic," he might say. "Go run around the block a few times" and "Put your fist in your mouth and swallow" were some of his more innocuous marching orders.

When he was at work in the tower, his language had to be indelible, inexorable, capable of bending spoons. Subtext, allusion, nuance, dramatic irony: these were the smithies upon which mistakes were forged. Thought had to be equal to articulation. No art. The kind of speech that lives relied upon. So many winged aluminum cartons of fragile eggs. Each of the, say, 250 passengers on each flight hanging unwittingly on each morpheme. Our father, Air Traffic Controller. He was that most avid reader, of auspices, time signatures and frequencies, topography and relief. Were he to nod off or blink, all heaven levitated might fall.

Discussing training conditions during the earlier period in the professionalization of air traffic control—the 1950s—McCartin writes, "At times the training regime could border on sadistic. As young developmentals handled traffic with a senior controller at their side, instructors would sometimes stand behind them, nattering in their ears, 'Why're you doing that? What was that for? Look at that guy!' Their purpose was to weed out anyone who could not handle pressure." This practice must still have been popular by the time my father reached the academy. I need only look at the evidence of my own upbringing. He seemed to have adapted his signature parenting style from the air traffic control training regime.

The controllers bonded in opposition to the administration under similar circumstances. McCartin quotes one disenchanted controller bemoaning the " 'father-son relationship' the F.A.A. had tried to cultivate between management and labor." The feeling was that, " 'like many fathers,' the FAA had 'failed to prepare for the day when its sons would grow up.' " This feeling, I know it well.

With the paranoia of an ailing patriarch, the FAA gave psychological evaluations that controllers resentfully referred to as "psycho tests." These tests, given as late as 1965, were intended to flush out social and emotional nonconformists

who, presumably damaged by the stresses of training and pro-
longed "development" on the job, might disrupt the delicate
ecosystem of the tower. As McCartin notes, controllers were
required "to take a written personality test . . . If they scored
poorly, they were scheduled for a psychiatric evaluation. If that
went badly, they could be disqualified from controlling air
traffic. Any controller who appealed his disqualification had
to pay the expenses of his case review." The purportedly objective "psycho tests" prompted controllers "to agree or disagree
with statements like, 'I admire the beauty of a fairy tale more
than that of a well-made gun.'" Considering that the people
who were attracted to, and could survive training for, a career
in air traffic control were often social and emotional nonconformists, these tests were widely understood to be coercive, if
not punitive.

The 1981 air traffic control strike was, among other things,
a case study in class ambition. As much as the conflict concerned actual working conditions, the strike was motivated,
too, by the desire to shift the public perception of air traffic
controllers and their work to match the high esteem the controllers had for themselves. They wanted to be recognized on
equal footing with pilots, as legitimate professionals.

Founded in 1968, PATCO relied on the star power of the
celebrity attorney F. Lee Bailey to lend it legitimacy. Bailey,
who would later serve as defense attorney for the likes of Patty
Hearst and O. J. Simpson, was a certified pilot, and thus familiar with and sympathetic to the hardships faced by controllers.
During negotiations with the FAA for recognition of PATCO,
Bailey pushed the organization's agenda in coded terms. He
assured FAA officials that controllers had no interest in rabble-
rousing. Bailey took pains to distance the organization from

the unsavory tactics used by other special interest groups like "Martin Luther King's march into Washington." PATCO was founded on a corporate model, with a board of directors, a president, and Bailey, as executive director. But the majority of rank-and-file members who resisted the word "union" for its working-class associations had working-class backgrounds, and few of them had more than a secondary education.

The earliest controllers were drawn from the ranks of the military, and the earliest officials of what would become the FAA were drawn from the ranks of journeymen controllers. The control tower has always had a military culture, which frames an uneasy relationship between the management and its workforce. By the late 1960s, as the job became more specialized and professional, recruiting efforts had increased the number of controllers with civilian backgrounds. Those new employees, who would be analogous to enlisted personnel and who now served under a class of government officials that likened itself to an officer class, had no clue about, nor inclination toward, the kind of deference such a relationship should entail. Seen from the other side, the rookies were offensively ignorant of military bearing. They didn't wear ties. Some even responded to orders by first asking "Why?"

These new civilian controllers formed what, for that time, was a diverse workforce: merit among them was determined not by pedigree or seniority but by swagger; the less likely one was to blink or flinch or allow oneself to be punked, the more that person could be trusted on the job. Though insufficient in the eyes of the old guard, it was a kind of discipline, that façade, a kind of bearing. In 1985, my father, still in the public eye four years after the strike, described the job for the Montreal *Gazette* using a revealing metaphor: "It was like you were a gunfighter and it was always high noon. You strap on the guns, fan back the jacket, grab the microphone and see how many you can stand."

———

On September 3, 1981, a local paper quoted my father speaking at a labor rally in support of PATCO. Reminding his audience of Reagan's pedigree as a union boss (Reagan was president of the AFL-CIO-affiliated Screen Actors Guild from 1947 to 1952, and in 1959 and 1960), my dad told the sympathetic crowd in Elizabeth, New Jersey, "We want to send a message to the former union president who occupies the Oval Office. If you crush PATCO, we know our union could be next." Speaking to the *Socialist Worker,* one of the few papers still supportive of the by-now-abandoned strike, his tone was similarly prophetic:

> The vast majority of the people have to understand what's going on here—union busting tactics being used against 12,000 highly skilled workers. If they don't, it sounds the death knell for unionism. I mean what's being done right now will be the precedent for all labor/ management struggles. If they can fire all of us and cavalierly say they're "going to rebuild the system," what does this mean to semi-skilled and unskilled labor that relies on the union for their strength and negotiating and bargaining power?

But by mid-September, most otherwise sympathetic unions had already decided to pass on invitations to board PATCO's sunken ship. The International Federation of Air Traffic Controllers briefly considered, then abandoned, plans to support the strike. Canadian and Portuguese controllers staged a two-day boycott of U.S. air traffic, but American pilots and machinists kept their work schedules without interruption. On September 19, 1981, the AFL-CIO organized a Solidarity Day March on Washington, DC, as a token show of support. The government fined PATCO more than $28 million in damages to the airlines, and froze PATCO's $3 million strike fund, which was intended to supplement controllers' lost incomes during the strike. PATCO was bankrupt. The striking controllers were effectively reduced to a group of aviation enthusiasts.

Some twelve hundred striking controllers were rehired within a week of the strike—well short of the two-thirds of the entire workforce that a congressional committee recommended to restore air traffic operations to full safety. Some controllers interpreted the president's forty-eight-hour deadline to mean that they must report for work within forty-eight hours of their first *scheduled shift*. Because of rotating days off, there were some who finished their last shift the morning of Monday, August 3, before the president announced the deadline, and may not have been scheduled to work again until Wednesday, in which case, some successfully argued, they had until that Friday to report for work. These controllers had time to assess the damage, and rescue their careers. Still, returning controllers were deeply resented, and punished with the least desirable work shifts and assignments. The Reagan administration refused to consider any further reinstatements. In the four weeks following the strike, applications to the FAA for air traffic control positions exceeded forty-five thousand. For a sense of scale, before the strike, the FAA facility in Oklahoma City turned out fifteen hundred graduates per five-month course.

By the time President Clinton lifted the order banning former controllers from federal employment, it was impractical for many to return to a job they hadn't performed in twelve years. When, in a further effort to piece together the labor movement's broken shell, the Clinton administration supported a bill that would ban the use of permanent replacements in response to strikes, conservative opposition and a Republican filibuster shut the bill down in the Senate.

In addition to being blackballed from the only job their specialized training qualified them to do, controllers who refused the president's deadline faced repercussions at home. Families suffered. When school started that September following the strike, my seventh-grade history teacher assured me with spiteful glee that my father would never get his job back. Our family doctor began casually canceling appointments. Weeks after the president's announcement, my mother caught federal marshals following me around the neighborhood as I rode my bicycle to friends' houses to play.

The marshals knocked on our door one day when I was the only one home to greet them. I did not know where my dad was, but I knew not to help them try to find him. They spoke to me as if I had answered the door holding a knife to my own throat. As one of them showed me his badge I noticed the other behind him drawing the curtain of his sport jacket to reveal his badge, too, but I also got a glimpse of the service pistol harnessed under his armpit.

At the time of the strike, my mother was working as a graphic designer at a local print shop. When marshals parked outside the print shop in their black sedans, the owners of the shop were understandably spooked. Fearing repercussions, they let her go, apologetically. My parents converted our garage into an art studio and my mom devoted all her maternal downtime to a steady current of freelance work. We had no health or dental insurance, but within a year, this small business of hers had grown enough that she thought to move out of the home studio and into proper office space in nearby Willingboro Plaza. The move added a rent bill to our family expenditures.

One of her clients was the thrift store my father, no longer EWR-bound, opened in his old neighborhood in North Philadelphia. He called the store Reruns, in honor of his love for television. My mother designed a logo that featured my dad, airborne, sporting leotards with a cape flowing from his shoulders. Part Superman, part Santa with a sack of secondhand goods, my dad was indomitable. Some of the merchandise naturally found its way to our house: electronics, appliances, tchotchkes. Our closets smelled of other people's clothes.

My father was otherwise unemployed for a year before he took a job as a night watchman at a warehouse. He had gone back on the speaker's circuit, too, and landed high-paying dates at several colleges. In this time of resourcefulness under duress, we made the most of our rations of government cheese. It was a minor holiday, the day the cheese arrived. Big as a shoebox, the taxicab-colored block of cheddar played a large role in our diet. Grilled cheese sandwiches, yes, but gooey slabs topped all our carbs, too, as well as our burgers, eggs, and sauces. Government cheese went with all the groceries we claimed with our fistfuls of food stamps. Even when PSE&G turned off the heat and electricity, the cheese was there for us. We made do, the ceiling in our living room sooty from the fumes of a kerosene heater while, for lack of a fridge, we kept the cheese and other dairy products in a cooler that we dug into the snow outside the sliding glass door.

The adversity didn't seem entirely real to me, but few things did. I was a thirteen-year-old delusional with hormones. My parents sheltered me from their fears and frustrations, while Serendipity seemed to follow us on fairy wings, tapping our foreheads each night with its magic wand. The bank holding the mortgage on our house stopped sending the note for a while. My parents didn't go asking questions. A year and a half later, a bank executive called to say my parents' mortgage file had been discovered behind a filing cabinet. It was an administrative error, the bank official said, and my parents worked out an arrangement to make up the missing payments.

Still, I considered what the strike had cost my family. Eventually, my father landed what turned out to be a short-lived position, thanks to random drug testing, as a train dispatcher with SEPTA, the Philadelphia regional transit authority, where he first worked as a switchman manually transferring trains from one track to another. One icy winter night, I got to see the shack, no bigger than an ice-fisherman's, where he warmed his feet in front of a space heater. My mother, brother, and I took him soup and coffee. I was in high school, old enough to see shame in the creases of his face.

Although he would eventually become a train dispatcher for New Jersey Transit, and retire as a union representative for the American Train Dispatchers Association, there was a wounded quality he never quite shook. He joked, one night on the periphery of the dark rail yard, that he had taken his life's work back to its essentials: one track, one switch, one purpose.

The Minority Business
Consortium

Leon the Fourth, as my aunt Donna called him, her Princeton boyfriend—her *white* Princeton boyfriend—took her on long walks across the university campus to photograph architectural details, trees, and each other. They talked about civil rights and the war in Vietnam. Leon read poems to her. Whenever she came to Princeton, where Bob had moved after he divorced my grandmother, Donna allowed herself to imagine life with Leon in a house full of books and paintings. But Leon's parents wanted "the very best" for their son, as Leon said, which was his way of saying his parents would not approve of his relationship with my aunt. But each time she returned home to the Germantown neighborhood of Philadelphia, once among her old friends, she was more convinced than ever that she wanted a life of literature and adventure, of music and exotic foods. She wanted to go to college.

Bookish, inquisitive, and a romantic, Donna is the second of Bob's three daughters. My mother is the oldest. It seemed unlikely to Bob—whose own father insisted that he leave high school in the tenth grade—that Donna's inclinations would lead her to some leafy liberal arts campus. When she presented him with an acceptance letter to Hampton, in Virginia, he felt his suspicions confirmed. He was relieved, certainly, that he would soon deliver her to an institution that would take responsibility for her development in a way he felt he could not. But in Bob's estimation, Hampton was little more than a finishing school, a boarding school for black dilettantes, hardly a center of intellectual pursuit. For Donna, it was a chance to leave behind the emotional wreckage of her family life in the wake of her parents' divorce.

She got the idea to apply to Hampton when she returned home for her senior year at Germantown High. She set about reestablishing the tabs she had kept on various people and discovered that a boy she was interested in had graduated and gone to Hampton. Prior to her junior year, which she had spent at Princeton High School, she would have marked this as a net loss of inventory in the romance column. Now, the salient detail indicated that someone she knew had gone away to college. *If he could do it . . .* , she thought. Donna was pragmatic. In the dream where she enjoyed an easy and supportive intellectual partnership, she saw boys, like Leon the Fourth, but with fewer impediments, with whom she could maintain a life of the mind long after graduation. Without input or counseling, Donna applied to Hampton, and got in.

The staircase, which she climbed with her portable pop-up television in one hand and her rolled comforter in the other, led her toward her assigned room in the dormitory's providential arms. She was used to historic buildings in Philadelphia. But her residence at Hampton, Virginia-Cleveland Hall, opened a more immediate and cinematic window on the past. She imagined crawling out through one of the dormer windows of the mansard roof to sit with a glass of wine—nothing fancy, she told herself—to watch the nineteenth century mingle with the twentieth in the quad below. The girls, imagined and real, all of them so pretty, from Tulsa and Shaker Heights, Chicago and Jacksonville. The ghostly, imaginary ones adjusted their touring hats while the hems of their bustles and crinoline echoed the sibilant Chesapeake as they walked; their gaits matched by the corporeal girls, bare-legged in cut-off jean shorts patched with embroidered flowers and peace symbols and, occasionally, Rolling Stones lips. The boys, in their dark suits, she could see, holding reins on wagons while the shuddering horsepower of Benji Davis's bright yellow Corvette dissipated that mirage, spitting gravel from beneath its steel-belted radials. She couldn't separate the strains of Earth, Wind & Fire rolling across campus from the three-part harmony of the gospel choir in her mind.

She met her new roommate, Trudy, and learned Trudy's parents were both ophthalmologists. "Ophtha-*what*?" asked Donna. As Trudy and Donna exchanged bits of their home lives, Donna couldn't help weaving in references to her Ivy League boyfriend and her father, a businessman in Princeton— not because she was proud of either, but because it would help justify why Donna should be accepted into Trudy's orbit.

The images Donna conjured of Trudy and her parents and the lives they led were so clear she could already imagine herself explaining to friends in Philadelphia exactly what the difference is between ophthalmology and optometry when they would inevitably presume wrong the branch of medicine her new imaginary parents practiced. *No, no, I'm sorry.* She rehearsed silently. *It's a common mistake, really. People confuse the two all the time. It's nothing to be embarrassed about.*

Donna wanted Trudy to tell her more about her dream parents. *Don't you have to have like seven years of school to become a doctor?* Donna asked. At least. And that's in addition to college, but when you're dealing with people's lives, you have to get used to the idea that you're always learning. *Always learning.* The phrase caught on a hook in Donna's dream and billowed out like laundry on the line.

By the time Donna started unpacking, Trudy had already outfitted her dresser top like the cosmetics counter at Wanamaker's. Her bookshelf held a stereo with a built-in eight-track player; its tuner filled a horizontal tube with neon green as it dialed along the frequency band. Donna set her seven-inch pop-up black-and-white television on her desk, proud that she had something to contribute to the collective media array. With each book Donna shelved on her side of the room, she glanced over to compare its heft with the crisp volumes of Harvard Classics Trudy had neatly arranged beneath her stereo. Donna's dog-eared gathering of paperbacks—Vonnegut, George Jackson, Poe, Aristotle, Ayn Rand, and Alice Walker—suggested reading habits dependent on impulse and chance rather than guidance and interest.

At the end of the first week, she found the notice of nonpayment in her campus mailbox, and she knew that there hadn't been a mistake. The next day she stopped in at the bursar as the notice requested. The matronly financial officer tried to calm her and offered to call her dad. Donna could picture all the mannerisms accompanying her father's voice as she followed its singsong Philadelphia brogue rasping from the telephone receiver.

She let her eyes wander the bursar's office, where the typewriters ratcheted like cash registers. Filing cabinets lined an entire wall, and above them was only a photograph of Gerald Ford hung beside one of a man who could have been George Washington Carver or Booker T. Washington. In a tan suit? No, it must be the college president. Where do *his* kids go to college? The woman handed Donna the phone. *Daddy? Daddy, where's the money?*

The truth, which Bob couldn't tell his daughter, was that he had made such a show of being a *macher* in Princeton that he never filled out the student loan papers he and Donna picked up together from the bank in town. "Nothing is more important than your reputation," he told me once. His latest venture, the Minority Business Consortium, had been profiled in *The Princeton Packet*. His stature was rising, and he wanted to prevent any interference with the illusion.

The *Packet* article from 1972 describes the MBC as a "miniconglomerate," and places the term in unattributed quotation marks. Either the journalist is being ironic or the term was pulled from Bob or Bob's promotional materials. The MBC literature is quoted: "a minority-owned corporation dedicated to the singular concept of developing and consolidating independent minority concerns into an effective, viable group capable of competing with established majority owned businesses for a realistic share of the American economic pie." The anchor business in the MBC was Bob's primary company, the Parham Group, a consulting firm dedicated to helping large corporations cultivate women and minorities for employment.

Though his pitch to women and minority candidates was to stay invisible, act grateful, and don't make mistakes. Another of the "half dozen small companies" in the MBC was the "artistic and graphic design company in the Philadelphia area called Marion Designs," my mother's studio. As an umbrella firm, the MBC provided assistance in "market analysis, management training, advice and encouragement." And, as the *Packet* quotes from another MBC publication, "MBC is a family service. The founder of MBC (Parham) has 25 years of street corner experience dealing with the bitter problems of hardcore ghetto inhabitants."

———

The building at 92 Nassau Street in Princeton is a unique feature of the streetscape. At the corner of Nassau and Witherspoon, its Tudor design, with decorative display of intersecting half timbers, steeply gabled dormers, and mullioned windows lacks only a thatched roof and is unlike any other building in town. Among the bookstores, coffee shops, and eateries that occupy the storefronts along Nassau Street are banks and upscale clothiers, jewelers. From his second-floor office, Bob would have looked down on this street scene busied by students in blazers and cable-knit sweaters, pastels and plaids and skinny ties, as well as those in small groups shrouded in the mystique of foreign tongues, and shoppers lingering or purposing on with their day, few if any of them black. He would have mused out that window, across the university lawn toward Nassau Hall, once, briefly, the seat of government for the liberated American colonies, while composing his own declaration.

"The families of MBC affiliates will have access to counseling on matters which threaten to undermine the family structure. A growing business man, like a growing tree, needs roots." The bravado in his rhetoric, and the certain knowledge that he could barely keep the light bill paid in his office, reveals the frustration and shame he must have felt shooing away his daughter in her time of need.

———

Again, Donna asked where the money was. Again, he feigned surprise. "How am I supposed to know where you're getting the money? It's *your* tuition!" His responses became aggressive and irrational. *I don't have any money,* he'd say. And *You wanted to go to Hampton, you figure it out.* And *You should have thought all of this out before you got there.* The truth was that he believed completing a loan application at any bank in Princeton would have given everyone in town access to his financial records. He was convinced the men he relied upon for ambient shine and prestige would have abandoned him and his dubious conglomerate if they knew how thin his coffers actually were.

Hearing this exchange put the financial aid officer at the Hampton Institute in caregiver mode, and she promised Donna they would figure out a way to buy some time, at least. From that moment, Donna was "Sugar" and "Sweetheart," and other confectionary endearments. But these were not consoling. Donna couldn't even look at the woman. Hearing each pet name made her want to scratch the woman's eyes out.

Donna couldn't bear the sight of Trudy or those pristine books like a stack of hymnals. She couldn't bear the sound of her eight-track tapes or the awful hum and ratchet of Trudy's flip clock. When Trudy suggested Donna call her mother in Philadelphia for the money, Donna mused a moment. She turned to face Trudy. "I want to scratch your fucking eyes out." She apologized immediately. But it felt good, just to speak her mind. If manners could no longer hide who she was, she decided, then she had no patience for anything but the most perfunctory human decency.

She tried to steady herself, to cast her thoughts ahead toward completing the semester, but it was, admittedly, a waste of time. She wanted to hide. The uppermost dorm window was inaccessible, but she had made a habit of crawling onto the fire escape outside the window of the fourth-floor landing in the stairwell. Two weeks—a kind of suspended animation—had passed and the weather was turning. She sat on the fire escape in the humid autumn night watching the ghostly tableau of history change frames as if she were clicking through slides on a View-Master disk, and she felt, well, bored. Without waking Trudy, Donna unplugged her television and carried it back to the opera box she had made of the fire escape. She hadn't thought to bring an extension cord and sighed heavily with the tiny screen staring up like a hungry child from her lap. Digging her thumbnail under it, she lifted the battery cover, but the batteries wore a lather of erosion. First, one battery shot into the coastal air, flashing like a fishing lure in random shafts of electric light woven through the yellowing leaves. Then another, until the case was empty. But the screen still held its doleful cataract upon her so she heaved the whole thing overboard as well. It landed with the clamor of a car wreck. It echoed through the acoustic night. Donna recognized the voice of every girl who called out one by one as lamps waking in dorm rooms began to illuminate the quad. She followed the voices' sleuthing logic as it unfolded: Was it a burglar? Did someone trip in the dark trying to sneak back into the dorm? She spent the remainder of the semester in the infirmary until a classmate offered to put up the money for her bus ticket home to Philadelphia.

Cartography

The problem of my adolescence, it seemed, was the yellow line. Toward the end of the driveway, my skateboard lay on its side like a capsized tanker. Beyond that, the solid yellow line. Like the stripe down a coward's back, it divided Twin Hills Drive, the sinuous main road bisecting Twin Hills Park, our subdivision in Willingboro, to establish an unofficial border between two hoods.

"The Nubian God" often cracked on me 'cause I lived on the east side of Twin Hills. He said that because I lived on the east side, I lived in the ghetto, the barrio, the favela. On the west side, see, there were no sidewalks. Uninterrupted lawns gave the homes a bucolic, stately mien. Cross Twin Hills Drive, though—cross that solid yellow line—and in addition to the urban appurtenance of sidewalks, you'd find a vague but discernible reduction in cachet.

Today, for once, Nubie didn't flaunt his status as he usually would by asking, for example, how my people were getting along, or if aid was getting through to our backward and "internecine villages" in the east. When he saw me eyeing the skateboard like a stray that had been following me around, he asked if there was any news on my ride yet. Until recently, I'd been the proud owner of a moped, make and model unknown. The seat was patched with black electrical tape and I'd sprayed parts of the chrome with silver acrylic to cover the rust, and cut contact paper designs out with stencils I got from the hobby shop to decorate the gas tank. I paid for the moped with money I earned, and I rode it, avoiding major thoroughfares—as I assured my mom I would—to the school pool or to the library or to my guitar teacher's house. Or to play Ping-Pong with the Nubian God.

Over the previous Christmas break I'd worked at CVS in the Burlington Center Mall. What I didn't spend on cassette tapes and magazines, I was required to deposit in a passbook savings account, as I wasn't yet of legal working age. I wasn't street legal for the moped either, but my mom was a graphic designer whose ability to counterfeit documents would have suited her for life in a clandestine radical movement. Instead, she rescued our family from run-ins with bureaucracies that were only going to tell us what we didn't want to hear. An inspection sticker, for example, to hold us until we could afford to replace the cracked windshield, or a pool badge when I lost the one I signed for on the last day of school. She changed dates on school forms and insurance cards. And when I needed to prove I was old enough for a work permit, she doctored my birth certificate. That any one of these might constitute a felony was no deterrent. We weren't strangers to confrontations with G-men.

By 1982, a year after Reagan fired him and thirteen thousand of his fellow air traffic controllers for engaging in an illegal strike against the federal government, my blackballed father seemed stuck in a daisy chain of shitty jobs, and dedicated himself instead to smoking weed. An otherwise zealous

imitator, I had difficulty reconciling this new ethos of surrender with his former occupation. Dad was hors de combat and
I, too young to imagine either rescuing my captain or assum-
ing his command, simply idled in resentment. Nube had had
no inkling of this larger, existential dread, but his knack for
reading people showed in moments when he distracted me
with questions—in this case, by asking me how I'd get to my
guitar lessons. Small talk. Uncharacteristic.

More characteristic was the elegant way he could tear people down. Kids who couldn't keep up with the improvised cruelty of Nubie's insults in a busting match would grasp at easy
jabs or lumber after him with some unimaginative reference to
his skin tone. He was black, and he identified as black, but he
was from a light-skinned family that subverted racial catego-
rization by maintaining, like the mere splash of vermouth in
their nightly cocktails, a bloodline barely redolent of Africa.
"Weak!" we'd shout at an overconfident homeboy reduced to
calling him Casper or Snowflake, and throw our hands down
as if we were done with the whole thing. It amazed me how
automatically people—regardless of race—would indict him
for racial noncompliance like it was the dirty secret, the worst
thing a motherfucker could think to say.

Though "tightly curled," Nubie's nearly blond hair and
khaki-colored eyes prompted strangers behind him in line
at the 7-Eleven to tap him on the shoulder and ask what he
was. His ability to attract that kind of attention fascinated me,
how his existence would confound even the most liberal racial
logic. He parlayed this mystique into a talent for making time
with girls, which I further fabulized into legend. It helped that
he was a full year older than me, even though we were in the
same grade. This was the result of his missing the cutoff date

for starting school by one week, and my having tested out of kindergarten. *Your mom so dumb she played hooky a whole year and told people she skipped a grade.* While Nube was smoothly growing into his role, my self-image was caught in a bitter custody battle between Alex P. Keaton and Jimi Hendrix. I had difficulty branding myself, and I couldn't blame girls for not knowing what to make of me. In my way, I resisted social conventions. But unlike Nubie, I was just not a popular kid.

It's not like I could think of a whole lot to throw at Nube either (other than calling him the Nubian God, which ain't no better than Casper, now that I think of it). But I thought I was at least idiosyncratic in my busting style when I did; and thought knowing words like "idiosyncratic" could make up for my not being funny. *Your mom's feet so crusty, she gets her shoes from a blacksmith.* Problem was, I wasn't so much funny as I was mean. *Your mom so dumb she got fired from Amway.* This was our bond, I suspect. Some guilt over our precocious pining for the world beyond our provincial borders gave us both a burden of awareness that felt immodest and, as with our newly big feet, made us self-consciously clumsy.

No—no idea how I'll get to my guitar lessons, I told Nubie. The fact was, I was already assed out over the question of how I'd continue *paying* for the lessons, since the money I earned from working at the CVS store in the mall was running low. Nubie tossed my Ping-Pong paddle from the milk crate where we stored the equipment.

As if flipping an omelet, I tapped the ball a few times into the air. I felt the tension almost elasticized as the ball heaved against its own inertia only to be sucked back into the open mouth of my paddle. Nube, standing there quietly, seemed as

fascinated by the fact of gravity as I was. I could feel his attention gathering like a cloud of gnats over my shoulder. "You
know how when you lose something you start thinking you see
it everywhere?" Nube said. "That raggedy thing wasn't even
mine, but now every black moped I see reminds me of yours."
I turned around to see what he was seeing: Tyrone.

Motherfucker.

Tyrone was one of Herman Joiner's four little brothers. The
only interaction either Nube or I'd ever had with any of the
boys in that family was a snowball fight one day when I was
helping Nubie shovel his driveway. (Instead of paying us for
shoveling, his mom would take us to the Pennsauken Mart,
where I once bought a wave brush, which I intended only to
display in my back pocket, because outside my mother's field
of vision I'd occasionally sport a do-rag in pantomime of
urban black machismo.) I remember there was a plush thud in
the thick of foot-high snow beside me, and when I looked up I
could make out the scurry of bodies behind drift-covered cars
across the street. We knew they were only fucking with us, but
because of our shared contempt for them, Nube and I were
easy to provoke. At least I was.

The more I heard them cackle with glee, the more wild-eyed
and iced with rage I became, returning dense missiles of snow
all the more desperately. I scared the shit out of myself when
such minor provocations would light a match in the dark basement of my mind where the whisper of voices sounded like a
gas leak. I hadn't yet noticed a pattern in what would trigger it,
this hysterical anger. A fly in the room, maybe. Or a basketball
caught between the rim and the backboard. It was bad.

Sometimes my little brother, Robbie, would attack me after
one of my spells of relentless berating had finally broken him.

My embittered homilies coaxed a similar indignation from the basket of my brother's gut. He'd swing at me uncontrollably. He was four. I worried he'd hurt himself, and the futility of his rage filled me with shame. It was all I could do to straitjacket him with my arms. The two of us then sobbed like a couple of drunks fumbling for the melody of a song we could not name. I sobbed that winter day, in rhythm with each snowball I launched at the glare-shrouded silhouettes across the street— Tyrone and his brothers.

The summer sun thickened the air of Nubie's garage. I felt the bile in my throat, my inner ear was full of that snake charmer's pipe again. Tyrone had done little to disguise my moped beyond, I could only assume, Sharpie-ing over my contact paper designs on the gas tank. There was nothing more to say.

My skateboard reeled in the streets like a length of garden hose. I knew the layout, the inner lives, in shape if not in detail, of almost every house in Willingboro because they were all based on just the handful of models that Levitt modified to various degrees from one park to the next. The parks were organized to suggest distinct neighborhoods, but their controlled arrangements conjured up little more than the impersonal logic of a Monopoly board, reflecting simple gradations in class and aspiration.

Levitt and Sons was the name of the company run by Bill Levitt. Bill, the founding father of our town, made the cover of *Time* in 1950. The Henry Ford of real estate development, he'd started with three built-from-scratch towns: the famous Levittown on Long Island; the one in Pennsylvania, across the

Delaware from where I grew up; and my own in New Jersey. Except because our Levittown had been partially mapped onto an already existing municipality, the township kept its original name of Wellingborough, or close enough.

Having built some twelve thousand homes, Bill Levitt and his brother, Alfred, put the first Willingboro homes on the market in 1958. Although the Federal Housing Administration insured mortgages in Levitt's development, which meant the development could not be legally segregated, Levitt insisted that permitting home sales to black families would deter white families from buying—a segregationist policy that finally succumbed in 1960, when, following his attorneys' fruitless appeal to the New Jersey Supreme Court, the first black family moved in.

None of this history was evident in the daily life of Willingboro as I knew it. Except for the increasing numbers of churches and synagogues that were either shuttered or converted to house fish-fries and places where folks could dance the "Macarena" in rented formal wear, there was little indication a revolution was taking place. In 1980, 43 percent of Willingboro's population was black, and the total population of the township was in decline. The closing of John F. Kennedy High School in 1989 concentrated the town's talent in Willingboro High School, giving "Boro" a music program without rival in South Jersey. The gospel singer Tye Tribbett and the R&B group City High are notable alums. By 2010, African Americans would make up more than 70 percent of the population.

If you were a student in the mid-eighties at a high school in, say, Cherry Hill or Mount Holly, or any other neighboring town, and played "first singles" (the top seed on your school's tennis team), I'd have been the only black kid you encountered the whole season, the one whose ass you likely whooped. Willingboro, home of Olympic gold medalist Carl Lewis, fielded indomitable teams in track, football, and basketball, but the tennis courts had already enjoyed their last resurfacing by the time I graduated. Although it was still very diverse, Willingboro Township was transforming, overtaking even centuries-old towns like Lawnside as the black middle-class stronghold of South Jersey.

In 1967, sociologist and University of Pennsylvania professor Herbert Gans published his study of Willingboro, *The Levittowners*. "As in other racially integrated areas," he claimed, mocking the language of his interviewees, "there is much speculation about the future, and a few people predict the early arrival of 'Philadelphia slum dwellers.'" This was hardly even coded. My parents, though, behaved more like immigrants than former slum dwellers, and I, a first-generation "Afro-American," considered myself the rightful heir to Levitt's prized demographic.

My parents had fled the proximity of their parents in the Germantown section of Philadelphia to stake claim in this Lotus Land of vernacular tract housing. Philadelphia became the place idealized in my memory. I marveled at how local children managed the summer heat with a hydrant instead of a swimming pool. There was one playground at the top of Widener Place, the street where my mother had grown up and where Mom-Mom Sarah still lived. But the basketball court there seemed eternally frosted with shards of broken glass, and the rusted merry-go-round might as well have had a mule hitched to it to draw water from some ancient, bilgy sluice. The playground served the housing projects, and there was an unspoken rule that I was not to cross the boundary indicated by the stark change in architecture between the neighborhood's humble row houses and the monotone façades of public housing. Before the projects behind my grandmother's house were built, some people in the neighborhood had kept chickens and raised vegetables in the open field. I pictured the people who'd occupied that land wearing bib shirts and shoe-buckle hats, and bartering with natives in feather headdresses. On the walls of my grandmother's living room were framed photographs of Martin Luther King, Jr., and John F. Kennedy, who, I had no question, were the founders of Philadelphia.

Despite my aloofness from the families recently drawn from the city to the sapling and sod hillocks of our Willingboro, I understood them. It was said that it takes three generations to produce gentility, and they were busy doing just this. Families like the Joiners, on the other hand, bypassed the urban acculturation period entirely. They arrived straight from the rural sticks in just one generation, short-circuiting the narrative of racial progress as I understood it. They weren't pulling themselves out of a slum. They had a taste for lawn gnomes and pinwheels that offended my budding sense of decorum. They were impossibly foreign to me, and that obscurity provided an easy screen for my most monstrous projections.

———

All night I schemed a course to the Joiners' yard to retrieve my moped. Calling the police wasn't an option, because I was not sure how the kid I'd bought it from came into possession of the moped in the first place. The deal was brokered by this other kid I met outside the school pool. Dude said he knew where I could get a cheap moped when he saw me admiring his. There was a paranoid urgency to the arrangement. Now, as I plotted my revenge, the last thing I wanted to consider was the possibility that the moped I bought might have been stolen from Tyrone, or that Tyrone might have known the person to whom it belonged. The whole way home from Nubie's I spent discrediting the scenario in which Tyrone, walking by my house, had noticed the moped on my porch and recognized it as his own. We lived on a cul-de-sac, I reasoned, and so there was no way Tyrone could have "coincidentally" glimpsed the moped. No, the only circumstance that might explain his wandering into visual range of my porch was if he was roaming the streets after curfew, looking for trouble. It did not occur to me that he might have watched from a window as I rode it up the driveway of Nube's house, directly across from his, any day during the few summer weeks before this.

Only one of the five Joiner family boys, Herman, was of driving age, despite the small fleet of vehicles in their driveway. There was an old conversion van that stood in the pooling rubber of its flat tires gathering pine needles; there was a dented moss green F-150 touched up in several places with primer and a sparkling lime green paint; there was a champagne Seville with a sloped rear trunk, and a rotating cast of economy cars that must have been won at auction because there were usually numbers written in grease pencil on the side window and temp tags in the rear.

They lived in a model called "The Gramercy," a two-story colonial with four bedrooms and a two-car garage. It was a color my dad would have called "doo-doo brown," with caramel shutters and navy blue trim around the doors and windows. Had the mother ever harbored ambitions of tending a flower garden, she'd long since abandoned them; a few random twiggy shrubs were the only plants to prong the well-packed dirt skirting the house. The garage doors were occasionally left open during the day, giving view to an assortment of dirt bikes and quads. What anyone in that family would need with my misfiring, oil-burning, third-hand-at-best moped was beyond me, and yet there he was, Tyrone, pushing my ride through every thought in my mind—my ride, which came nearly up to his chest, so that, as he wheeled it around the house and into his backyard, he looked, in the image congealed in my memory, as if he were bulldogging a heavily drugged steer into the chute for slaughter.

———

Midnight expeditions with Nubie—"rambling," as we called it—had always been exciting because we were breaking curfew. We didn't have an agenda. We were just bored. Unlike Tyrone, we had no interest in breaking any ordinances other than curfew itself. It was as simple as a game of tag: don't get caught.

First Nube and I pool-hopped at school pools. Then one night Nube brought a guest to our one-in-the-morning meeting place, the band shell in Broido Park. This was the park where Debbie T. would soon teach me to tongue kiss; the park where I would hear live music for the first time from musicians not wearing tuxedos. Anyway, Nube had with him that first night the knuckleheaded Iranian kid who lived on the next street down the hill behind Nube's. After that, our crew grew incrementally, and soon resembled a pack of zombie-eyed preteens wild with the night's musk, liberated from our circuits between school and ColecoVision consoles. That's when I knew enough to bail.

Here's proof God loves fools and children: the first night I chose to stay home was the night the ramblers broke protocol and decided to throw pebbles at some late-night beer-drinking rednecks. This was a couple of weeks before summer break, and we were all impatient with school. Someone was bound to act out. When Nube appeared in school the next morning with his nose taped and both eyes blackened, I didn't care if anybody called me a pussy for having bailed. The gossip that went around later in the day was that police had rounded up all the kids who were out that night—and some who weren't—after they caught the Iranian kid and forced him to name names. It gave me great material for busting on Nube, but nobody but him got to hear it because Nube's parents didn't allow him out of the house for the whole summer. Because my name miraculously hadn't appeared on the Iranian kid's list, I was the only person allowed to visit Nube at home, which is how we got so good at Ping-Pong.

Like practice runs, those earlier outings had served me well after all. There was a system in place and I knew it. I knew whose parents stayed up late watching television, which empty nests were shut up tight like beach houses in the off-season. As I made my way to the Joiners' to repo my ride, I knew which yards I could safely cut through, staying off the street and out of the lights. I'd even thought to leave the screen to my bedroom window open to avoid the shush and click racket of raising it. There was only the shudder of the window frame in the sash, and the flash of my Jack Purcells disappearing over the sill.

I vaulted out the window and crouched behind the forsythia to survey the street. Shadows swaying like kelp played over my neighbor's Trans Am parked in the street, condensation pebbling its broad rear window. The voice of Johnny

Carson echoed from bedrooms as if the whole neighborhood were a well-dispersed drive-in theater. I took the fenceless cut-throughs. I didn't want to risk disrupting lullabies with the shimmer-clang of a chain link under my leaping 115-pound frame.

Originally, fences were prohibited in the Long Island Levit-town. Open and accessible common space was meant to foster cohesion among residents. This must have been one of Alfred's ideas. It was for just these sorts of kumbaya design features that Bill Levitt muscled his little brother out of the family business. By the time he broke ground on Willingboro, his last development, Bill couldn't give a rat's ass whether or not residents felt like they lived in a cohesive community. He owned a big-ass yacht.

One longer-lived feature of the two previous Levittowns was the successful exclusion of Negroes (as opposed to the unsuccessful, if also fervently pursued, efforts to keep out Jews). I'm not speculating which prohibition the Levitt Cor-poration dispensed with first in those communities preceding Willingboro—the prohibition on fences or the prohibition on Negroes—but at least in my own mind, the two have a syl-logistic relationship. What conditions allowed Willingboro, in contrast to nearly every other municipality in Burlington County, to become such a haven for middle-class black fami-lies? Maybe residents decided fences were a good idea after all when they found out who was moving in. Or maybe it was the installation of fences that disrupted, as Alfred might have predicted, the bonding process among neighbors enough to give black home buyers a chance to slip through those divided ranks in increasing numbers without lighting up the phone trees. Whether they were intended to wall in or wall out, though, fences were the norm in Willingboro. It was so rare to find a fenceless yard, I figured that the household must be philosophically committed to accessible common spaces, idealists hoping to ride out a downturn in the market of human sociability, and these folks would surely welcome my trespass anyway.

The kind of stockade fences I encountered at the Joiners' generally guarded a swimming pool, so I expected to find a kidney-shaped sheen at the center of their yard, dark as a tar pit in the night, or a precipitous cedar ledge surrounding an aboveground pool, its fiberglass pump half-successfully obscured by a trellis with potted ivy. But upon climbing the only tree with a limb high and strong enough to reach from their neighbor's side yard out over the Joiners' fence, all I could see was a large patch of dirt spreading just beyond the shed in the corner to the right of the sliding glass door. The shed must have been made by Mr. Joiner himself, because it looked more like something out of a documentary about life in a shantytown than anything purchased off the sidewalk outside Rickel's hardware.

There it was, teetering on its stand by the rear door of the garage to the left of the kitchen's sliding glass door, partly disassembled—my moped. Shimmying out to where the tree limb dipped and then braced against the top of the fence, I let myself drop into the spiky arms of one of the yew bushes lined along the perimeter. Just as I did this, I heard the sliding glass door open like the lid on a can of baked beans.

Whoever opened the door, thank god, was too distracted with the dog being let out to notice the top of the bush I'd fallen into flapping in the shadows across the yard. I tried to keep everything still as I stared up at clouds bright as teeth in a black light nightclub, but couldn't resist peeking out to see Mr. Joiner clip the dog's collar to the nylon leash. Who the fuck would keep a Pomeranian on a leash in the yard?, I wondered. Though he did seem happy to be there, the little fluff-ball, bright and curious as he spotted what his master had not. He was quiet about it, too, the dog. It was our secret. I liked the little fucker. Finally, Mr. Joiner tracked back into the house, and, like a roach, I scrambled around the yard, out of sight.

I couldn't tell which parts went where, so many of them were laid out on a bedsheet on the ground beneath the moped. The seat and gas tank had been removed and now leaned in the shadows against the house. Although it was dark and there was no evidence of this, I was certain Tyrone was preparing to repaint my moped properly. At least in the dark, there was nothing to suggest this was *not* my moped. Then again, reassembling it was well beyond me. I would have to repossess the moped and take it to the bike shop to get it back in working order, which would surely cost me more than the thing was worth to begin with. I had to abort the mission in the hope that when I *did* get my ride back, Tyrone would have it running better than it had before he stole it.

Trying to sort all of this out in the Joiners' yard, I was distracted and couldn't focus. I couldn't help myself. I had to pet the dog. And then it occurred to me.

———

She wasn't even barking, just licking me and squirreling around in the hammock of my rugby shirt. She pecked my face with the end of her cold little muzzle as, trotting, I connected the shadows between each yard, the moon coating treetops and lawns in that palest particulate as I retraced my route home.

I skirted Broido Park and turned north onto Topeka Pass, up the incline defining one half of Twin Hills' eponymous, if overstated, topography. Here was where I famously busted my ass in fifth grade. When I told my mother I wanted a skateboard, the first thing she did, after kidding me about aspiring to be the first black professional skateboarder, was buy me a book on the basics of skateboarding. Before she consented to buy me a board, I had to give her a summary of what I'd learned after each chapter. The chapter on falling still stands out in my memory—how to do so without breaking my neck, that is—because it was this hill and my failure to apply what I learned from that chapter that ended a promising skateboarding career before it even began.

Back in my room, I scraped together a pile of dirty clothes with my foot and balanced the dog on the top, like a figurine, but she was more interested in exploring her new surroundings. I left her sniffing around as I drew the door shut and backed out of the room. Because of our furry little houseguest, poor Dudley had to sleep in the yard that night. Fortunately, he usually slept in the kitchen anyway, so I was able to usher him out the sliding glass door without much fuss.

Dudley was a collie-lab mix—the kind of dog certain kinds of people like to collar with bandanas. People like my mother. A pegboard in the laundry room was stocked with dog-lover's hardware. I retrieved one of Dudley's old double bowls and one of the half-dozen leashes hanging there. Thus provisioned for the night, I slumped to the floor on my elbow to play with the Pomeranian. In addition to giving her home address, her tag read "Kindred," and I was thinking that's a cool name—kind of soulful without being obnoxious, you know, like that my-soul-is-deep-like-the-rivers sort of black-folk pretension.

But I wondered if it could work for a human, and I began meeting various imaginary black people named Kindred, trying to determine whether or not I had an urge to roll my eyes as I shook their hands. "Hey. Kindred. Whassup." Or, if it was a she and she was fine, "*Kin*-dred," I'd lilt before glistening my bottom lip as if it were the edge of an E-Z Wider. I'm ashamed to admit I spent time thinking about shit like this. The constant rehearsal of race.

Kindred made herself comfortable on the pile of clothes, and just in case, I hooked the little question mark of the leash onto her collar and slipped the loop handle under the leg of my desk chair. I slid the bowls of food and water closer to her.

It wasn't easy to sneak Kindred out unnoticed the next morning. My mom had let Dudley back in and he'd caught wind of the alien dog. So I put Kindred out my window, lassoing the leash over some branches on a bush. Before I told my mom I was going out, I called Nube to ask him to open his garage and wait for me there.

By the time I skated up my boy's driveway with Kindred inside my zippered windbreaker, Nubie was sitting in a chair orphaned from a long-gone kitchen set, clearly expecting an explanation as to why I'd gotten him up that early. "So I stole the dog," I reported.

"What dog?"

I lifted Kindred from my jacket and knotted the leash around the handle of the lawn mower. "The Joiners'."

"Shit, man—why'd you steal their dog?"

"I have a plan."

"When—wait, *how*?"

"I rambled last night. I was planning to steal back my ride, but your 'homie' over there had it all chopped up."

"You rambled? Alone? What, you were just going to, like, steal back your ride?"

"Yeah, but he had the spark plugs and shit all spread around the patio." I sprinkled imaginary parts around the garage floor at my feet to illustrate.

"So you took the dog instead?"

I put my hands on my hips, nodded proudly.

He sighed. "And when you need a safe house, it's me you think of?"

"Come on, I have a plan."

"Yeah? And I have a record. Don't tell me you were gonna ransom the dog or some shit."

My eyes tumbling around in my head like sneakers in a dryer while I tried to think of a plan, I untied Kindred. "No, dumbass, I'm giving the dog *back*. You know—like those firemen who start fires in order to be the hero?"

My friend struggled to make sense of all this. As did I. "I fail to see—" he started to say, but I cut him off.

"He'll know it's too much of a coincidence that I just *happened* to be the one who found the dog. Right? So, like, he'll know I'm sending him a message."

"Which is . . . what, exactly?"

"That I can take something of *his,* too." Mob logic for a thirteen-year-old. Only, my fantasy mob would always end up looking something like the board of trustees of a small nonprofit arts organization, cutthroat and vindictive but not exactly scary. Still, somehow it was like placing a horse's head right in Tyrone's bed. Or like when Tom Hagen, the Corleone Family's consigliere, sits in the courtroom gallery with the snitch's brother who wears a Giuseppe cap to show that he's fresh off the boat from Sicily and probably still smelling of goat. All it takes is the brother's presence to remind the snitch of the old-school code: *snitches open their own veins in a penitentiary bathtub*. Even in crime one may be compelled to surrender personal security for the greater good.

The dog, of course, would be unharmed here. But while the threat implicit in my returning her would be an empty one, I wanted him to know I *could* have.

"I think you're kinda overestimating somebody's intelligence," Nube mused. "Not saying *whose*." Scanning his garage then, I noticed bicycles that must have tumbled onto each other at some point over the last five years.

"It'll work, trust me. 'Sides, he's not stupid. I mean, he stole my ride right off the fucking porch."

I was in the middle of the street with the dog in my jacket when I heard Nube's garage door closing behind me. I got to the Joiners' driveway and looked back across the street. Nube was watching from his living room window. My demands were simple and direct enough that I didn't need to state them, but I rehearsed them in my mind so they would be written into the flex of every muscle on my face: I wanted my ride returned. I wanted some evidence that it had been unharmed. I wanted to see some goddamned contrition for the hardship, the hardships I'd endured.

A Moving Violation

On Christmas the year I turned sixteen, I unwrapped one of my smaller presents from under the tree to find a die-cast Hot Wheels car. My parents had a laugh. Once upon a time, my father promised to buy me a car for my sixteenth birthday. That birthday had come and gone a month before. My mother had been promoted to art director in charge of Pennsylvania Yellow Pages. We were hardly poor, but a third car in the family was still beyond my parents' means. The toy car was a joke. My dad believed that the greater the depth of disappointment he could provoke in me initially, the greater my experience of joy would be once he rescued me from that disappointment. They handed me a second gift, about the size of a jewelry box. When I opened it, I found a Chevy key ring with two keys on it.

"The keys to your new car!" they both exclaimed.

Still in our slippers, we all shuffled down the driveway, gripping our elbows like a chain gang set out into the cold. There, with a bow on the hood, was a ten-year-old Chevy Monza hatchback.

"Get in," my dad instructed.

Astonished, I was half-afraid to touch *my* steering wheel, *my* gearshift. He got in on the passenger side and lounged beside me, darkening my periphery like a bad conscience. I could have sat there all day marveling at that dashboard, its gauges crude as field instruments, so many tiny corners poignantly clutching the dust of the car's previous lives. Snow mounded high as the windows on either side of the driveway I'd shoveled just two days before. My mom went back into the house, but I could see her watching us from the kitchen window.

His breath obscuring his face like an anonymous source on *60 Minutes,* the old man told me to "start her up." We sat for a while and I squinted as I flicked on each blinker. First one eye, then the other, as if my own body were being emancipated, released into the male vernacular of manifolds and carbure-tors. From now on, there would be no denying my autonomy. I switched on the wipers; fingered the ashtray dimpled by a lost archive of flame. I dialed up the fan that blew a wind from the vents hard enough to scour my sinuses. "Well," he said expec-tantly. "Take her for a ride!"

I had completed driver's ed, but still didn't have a license, I reminded him. "Just as well," he said, "because you don't have insurance either." How, then, was I supposed to take "her" for a ride? I knew the answer. *Carefully.* I told myself this was my father's way of making sure I drove safely, that this was my father's way of caring. This may be true, but there was an additional truth. Honest people, the upstanding and obedi-ent, my father's lessons often implied, are leading riskless and therefore unrewarding lives. We, the exceptional, would not be subject to such limitations.

He got out of the car as I turned the key and the engine

stirred once or twice before coming to life. When he reached the porch, he turned and tapped the side of his nose—his signal that we now shared an understanding. Our secret was our bond. This was our pact. His eye twinkled as he ducked slightly, stepping back into the house.

Marine Boy

To psych myself up for Marine Corps boot camp, I drove half a mile north of the storefront recruiting office, to the video store in a competing strip mall, and rented *Apocalypse Now*. I'd signed the papers, and planned to overcome the ensuing fear of death by wading unflinchingly into the tropics on that screen in our den, big as a car windshield, its red, green, and blue lenses combining like searchlights on the mirror of the cabinet's opened lid.

Ahead of me were three months of basic training. I wasn't scared of the exercise, having been captain of my high school tennis team for two years. I was prepared, at least, in body. No, boot camp was scary because until then I'd only ever pretended at self-destruction. War was purely conceptual for me, the fact of my enlistment the only real cause I'd yet had for contemplating my mortality.

———

Within two weeks of my arrival on Parris Island, my paternal grandmother, Ollie, died. There was life insurance involved. So, my father, recipient of that money, bought a boat. Now, the reason I joined the Marine Corps was to get money for college. Let's just say I was confused and dismayed to find there was a financial need my father felt more pressing. If only to guard against the hives with which I typically responded to emotional stress, I had to make up a story that I could believe in, one that could make sense of my father's actions. "He came into some family money," I explained to people. It was a legend I tailored for exhibition, regalia for the humble-brag I'd begin by describing my father's new cabin boat, which I'd only ever seen in a photograph from below, dry-docked on a lift. Only sometimes was I forced to admit, to my immediate embarrassment, that my father had been so undisciplined as to blow fifty grand on a dumbass boat. The father I had so long idolized and I were becoming two very different people.

For what it's worth, these were unstable times, the tail end of "white flight" across America, but especially pronounced in my town. An unfortunate shorthand, "white flight" jumbles class and race by assuming all members of the escaping class were white, and that their egress was uniformly motivated by racial fears, but it is, give or take a few statistical outliers, largely appropriate. What remained of the pioneer homeowners in Willingboro was a smidgen of retirees with little or no stake in the school system, and a good number of households either blinded to race by their own enlightenment or comfortably disinterested in the declining value of their property. Or both.

My hometown had morphed in subtle and disorienting ways. Classmates who once measured themselves by their parents' hourly *rates* had been body-snatched and replaced by others who took pride in their parents' hourly *wages,* while rumored bonuses yielded to "windfall overtime" and "holiday pay." The average skin tone deepened by several shades, though we still wore neon-colored Izod shirts with our collars turned up, our sockless feet chafing inside cheap leather boat shoes. Many families just learning to put on airs were guilty of conspicuous errors, the driveways of their "Gramercy" or "Ardsley" model houses sentineled by concrete lions or plastic flamingos.

Some of us, more chameleonic than others, had refined our sense of striving, even if we had no real concept of precisely what it was we were striving *for*. I, for one, distressed by my folks' otherwise glass-ceilinged finances, devised ingenious yarns to revise that narrative, the way natives seek to explain a volcano's silence or pagans read motive into the motions of stars. I told stories that might foreshadow brighter futures than our demographics suggested. Our town had served as a stepping stone for so many families en route to tonier districts displacing the orchards and cornfields of South Jersey, but it was beginning to harden around me, and I wanted out.

I obscured how my father, despite his stumbling, lurching efforts to recover after losing his job in 1981, came to afford the twenty-four-foot Bayliner just out of its shrink-wrap. For the truth of his swift depletion of my grandmother's life insurance, unembellished, surely would have placed my father on a par with some lucky drunk at the racetrack.

Of course, with my father, I refused to acknowledge the boat, as if it were some floozy stepmom. I found his invitations to come aboard backhanded, a welcome that would serve only to lend him my witness so that he could better enjoy the funhouse spectacle of his own consumption, rattling off maritime trivia he'd learned from a bullshit course he'd taken at the marina.

How he got the boat was to his mind none of my business. Besides, it wouldn't have been enough money to get me through college. If it *had* been, and if, by some freak celestial alignment, (1) I had not gone off to boot camp that June after dropping out of college in a self-destructive funk; and (2) my father had not thought of using the money to repair his ego, still smarting from the strike's failure, and reward himself for having weathered, family and home intact, the intervening years of material deprivation—then I would have blown that shit anyway. Because the kid I was before boot camp? I wouldn't throw peanuts at that kid. This is not entirely true. I can talk tough now, but I'd recognize the boy's befuddled mien and offer him some kind of guidance.

———

As he frequently announced, my dad had long since fulfilled his obligation to the universe when one June evening of my eighteenth year, under the lights in Carl Lewis Stadium, I moved the tassel on my mortarboard from one side to the other. Not so long after that, with the forbearance of one retiring from a job he'd always felt beneath him, he set me, my duffel bag, my guitar, and a secondhand cube fridge on the curb outside Quad IV on the Rutgers Livingston Campus, and promptly drove away. Imagine his surprise, then, when, just a few short months later, he discovered me back home, as if waiting for him to dream up our next adventure: I had bailed on my second semester at Rutgers to save everyone the embarrassment of trying to pull it out of the fire.

It must have been late May because, even though I was not officially living at home, my dad and I had just opened the pool. Sean, a friend who'd graduated from Willingboro High

with me in '86, was back home, I remember. Seemingly minutes after commencement ended, Sean had left for Parris Island
just as he had always planned to. A year later, he was home
from 29 Palms to serve on recruiting duty. For this he needed
bodies to fill the seats at the Marine Corps Recruiting office in
the strip mall at the intersection of Route 130 and Beverly Rancocas Road. Sean gathered up the chronically unemployed and
a number of us who'd lasted little more than a semester in college, gathered us the way a preacher gathers winos and homeless people, with the promise of coffee and shelter in exchange
for our presence in the pews.

In high school I'd cultivated a pampered bad boy persona—
or tried to, anyway; scared of fashionable pharmaceuticals, I
was a stoner wannabe. I ran for class president and lost, court-
ing a constituency that I discovered, for all their huzzahs and
high fives, wouldn't actually vote. I'd joined half a dozen clubs
just to be around the girls they attracted and was cool with a
variety of crowds without being particularly popular in any of
them. I played guitar. I played tennis. I sang in the choir. I ran
track. I drank with those who drank in the woods behind the
school during free period, but then I parked alongside the AP
kids and stood on the hood of my car proclaiming: "To thine
own self be true!" without any idea whom or what I was quoting. Go ahead, cringe. Exceptional, I said. A piece of work,
said others. I was a floater on the surface of life, hesitant even
to place an oar in the water. And so, with mock courage, I cast
my tube in wherever the current was swift enough to catch
my eye.

Sean had always wanted to be a drill instructor. While
I didn't exactly admire this ambition, I was attracted to its
intensity (that attraction yet another symptom of the manic

depression I thought was merely a by-product of my devotion to Jimi Hendrix, but which I would many years later begin to puzzle out by connecting the genetic dots—great-grandfather, grandfather, mother, aunt, brother—of family members similarly afflicted). Sean's closest friend, Nate, had a hard-on for the air force, so I had always lumped the two boys together. They strode the halls of Boro High, Sean and Nate, wearing their "Aim High" or "Swift, Silent, Deadly" T-shirts with equal pride. Military was military, if you asked me. But then, I couldn't have told you the Marine Corps from the Drum and Bugle Corps.

When I asked who it was calling downstairs on the phone, Bob, my mother's father, said he didn't know; he hadn't asked. My mother must have given out the number. " 'Sup, Sean," I said a moment later, smiling into the receiver, and then cupping the mouthpiece while waiting for Bob to leave the room.

The tale of woe I'd begun telling myself was that my father had kicked me out of the house when I dropped out of college, and this was why I was practically homeless. The truth was that my relationship with my father had begun to fray as soon as a few hairs pushed through the skin on my chin. He needed the idea of his son to be distinct from the fact of the man passing him en route to the bathroom. I couldn't pull off such a performance because my body was just as alien to me as it was to him. Broke and staying in one of the upstairs rooms, a dusty unused part of my grandfather's house across town from my parents', I looked forward to even the smallest plot developments in life that might break the monotony of my days. I imagined Sean must be home for some kind of military spring break, and hoped there was an invitation to hang forthcoming.

Sean said he'd heard I left school, and was hoping to catch

up with me. Also he needed a few bodies. He said he had promised his "boss"—as if he worked at a car dealership—he could produce a few bodies a week in exchange for this recruiting assignment allowing him to come home for a month. Otherwise they would ship him right back to the Mojave Desert.

"For real, dude?" I said. "Damn, but . . . Fuck *that* shit."

"Twenty minutes, okay? That's all I ask. I can come over and pick you up, hunh?"

Couldn't leave my boy hanging.

———

The Marine Corps recruiter Sean was assigned to, a squat little master sergeant, seemed laughable in his little blue uniform, walking around the office all tight and jerky like he was constipated or something.

"Sean tells me you're only home a few weeks to regroup," he said, punctuating each phrase with a jut of his chin or an inverted nod. "I can sympathize, you know. It's tough. You're probably the first in your family to go to college, am I right? We usually don't have people at home to help us figure everything out—am I right?"

Every question was rhetorical, broadcasting its intended response, even when that response was in fact far from self-evident to me. "Last *I* checked college wasn't free," he continued. "*Somebody's* gone have to pay for it. Might as well be the government, ooh-rah."

I winced at the hayseed contraction with which he spoke the word: *gub'ment*. The "ooh-rah," too, was odd. He dropped it into his speech like "amen" or "praise God." He wasn't from the Northeast, I could tell, but he didn't seem to be from the Motherland either, that abstract and boundless place below the Mason-Dixon line where, I believed, ancient peoples still walked the red earth barefoot. If not the South, then somewhere in the Midwest maybe? Which was about as mysterious to me as Canadian football.

I was just a body making itself useful by staring vacantly at a man in a uniform. By the end of the recruiter's spiel—which turned out to be somewhat longer than twenty minutes—I had a handful of flyers and pamphlets and what I fully expected to be Sean's eternal gratitude.

Despite having been mercilessly turned out of my childhood home ("victim," in my self-conception, was fast replacing "rebel"), I still had keys to the front door, and felt like swimming. Sean drove me, in that Ford Taurus with its government plates, to my parents' house on Tinker Place, where I tossed all the pamphlets on the glass-topped dining room table, forgetting about them even as they left my hand, and then shimmied through the sliding door, making sure not to let the dog out. I snaked out of my T-shirt and kicked my sneakers off before seal-diving into the pool in my khaki shorts.

All the stuff of my life—my practice amp, my tapes, my notebooks—all of that was now at Bob's. Everything but the cube fridge. Bob, my mother's bachelor father, had given me a folding cot (he wasn't prepared for boarders) in the room overlooking the garage, which I set up by the window so I could indulge in the cigarette habit I'd cultivated at Rutgers. This was on Bolton Lane, one of two streets cut off from the rest of Buckingham Park by the four lanes and tree-lined median of Van Sciver Parkway, wedged in behind the Rancocas Hospital—the hospital where my brother, Robbie, had been born and where I had been laid up for two weeks with tubes up my nose after an asthma attack in fourth grade, the one time in childhood I could remember my father saying he loved me. Bob's house, a Cape Cod he'd taken over from my aunt Donna after her divorce, had been in the family almost as long as Tinker Place. Either address might appear under my name on a job application or an emergency contact form, and I had keys to both, a fact that did not prevent me from believing myself homeless.

Another friend had connected me with a temp agency, but whether out of boredom or depression I had a habit of just . . . walking off jobs. More than once I'd stood in line in the parking lot of some warehouse or tool-and-die shop to get a Saran Wrapped tuna fish sandwich, only to find myself overcome by a mild terror when I saw the workaday world rippling in the diamond-patterned stainless-steel siding of the truck. Even today, the sight of a lunch truck kicks my pulse up a notch. I'd find myself taking refuge in the bucket seat of the rusty Chevette Bob loaned me, jabbing presets on the dash radio before reaching to light the roach that was either in the ashtray or beneath the foil lining of my cigarette pack. I'd erase the thought of work altogether before driving back to Bob's. One more awful job successfully ditched.

In the wake of the air traffic controllers' strike, I had convinced myself of the nobility of the labor class. I still believe in that nobility—far more romantically, in fact, than I might had I aspired to it. Maybe my father's experience in the strike broke my faith in the power of solidarity and the ability of unions to secure a stable domestic life.

After my meeting with the Marine Corps recruiter, I hadn't much felt like going back to Bob's, back to my cot and the vale of cigarette ash I was accumulating in the windowsill beside it. My parents' house was, at least, clean; and the refrigerator reliably full. These small comforts were worth the risk of a run-in with my father.

Whenever my father found me in his house, the look on his face, some combination of smug and regretfully judgmental, said *Lay down your king—game over.* Being caught there with my head in the fridge only gave him additional grounds for the sort of chest-thumping displays he seemed to find so grimly satisfying. Thankfully, not having seen my dad's car in the driveway when Sean wheeled the Taurus onto Tinker Place, I was free to make myself at home.

Despite my asthma and developing taste for Marlboro Lights, my lungs were strong. I could drag myself through nearly three laps underwater before my chest felt like bursting. (Granted, the pool was only, like, twenty yards long; still.) As a kid I liked to wad sticks of Juicy Fruit in my mouth and sit at the bottom of the deep end, imagining I was no longer oxygen-dependent. *Marine Boy,* the anime cartoon, held me in such thrall that I was willing to risk committing my terrestrial form to the deep in order to glimpse the amphibian divinity nestled in my brain. The "oxy-gum" invented by Professor Fumble allowed Marine Boy to patrol the depths, keeping the ocean safe, alongside his friend Splasher the dolphin.

I had been daydreaming underwater with my back against the poolside. He must have been at the edge of the pool for a while. Coming up and reaching for the ledge, I inadvertently placed my hand on my father's foot as he crouched there, waiting. He was clutching the Marine Corps pamphlets. "This supposed to be some kind of joke," he grunted as he shook the fist of literature in my face like a rolled-up newspaper. Squatting only made his bulk that much more formidable, his broad shape blocking the sun.

"What?" I said, in a lame bid for time.

His strategy with me of late was to insist that I find regular, "gainful" employment. Just a few weeks ago it had become an outright ultimatum: if I didn't find a full-time job, he wouldn't allow me in his house at all. He'd given me some unrealistic deadline at the time—a week, perhaps—which I made a point of ignoring. Still, it took up a great deal of my energy to not think about the ultimatum.

He didn't have to know I had only agreed to *consider* the Marine *Reserves,* and not a *full-time* enlistment anyway. Sgt. Ooh-Rah had repeated "one weekend a month" so many times it had taken residence in my mind with all the logic of a public television pledge drive. *That's nothing,* I heard a distant voice in my head exclaim. Surely I could spare a few cents a day for my country. The pamphlets agreed: one weekend a month was nothing. A reservist would have to serve two weeks each summer, too, but that was mentioned so seldom it hardly even factored.

My father was afraid for me, I knew; just as he knew that if he expressed any form of disapproval, I might exploit his concern as a weakness.

"You wouldn't last two weeks in the Marine Corps."

———

It was *absolutely imperative* that I leave for boot camp in June, the Marine Corps recruiter told me. Otherwise, I would not be able to join the field communications training program, starting in September, which he said was the best job my middling ASVAB scores qualified me for. It didn't occur to me to ask to see my scores on this military placement test. Still, I was reluctant; starting in June would mean being in South Carolina in the three hottest months of the year—though it was the sand fleas, he said, not the heat, that would be the toughest part of boot camp. I soon enough found myself stepping in the yellow footprints painted on the roadside, outside the main doors of the Marine Corps Recruiting Depot on Parris Island, South Carolina.

I lasted two weeks. My platoon, 2069, waited to be issued rifles in the great hall of the armory, rank and file, still redolent of the civilian malaise we were shedding. Someone's way-leading sibling or cousin could have sent word of the impending tonal shift, for chrissakes. That information should have been filtering through our ranks like so much truth-telling samizdat. Yet somehow not *one* of us seemed to have had any warning that on this day, the two-week-mark shit was about to get real.

By now we were expected to have memorized the Lord's Prayer, which would come in handy as we began receiving a kind of activity-based time-out, whereby, instead of being sent to sit at the bottom of the stairs or on a stool in the kitchen, we would be sent "digging," which consisted of an especially punishing exercise routine. Throughout the island were either sandboxes or dirt patches bared in the grass, innocently paired with pull-up bars that looked rather like minimalist jungle gyms. During that original two-week honeymoon phase, the domination we suffered had been mostly mental; I did not yet understand that the pseudo-playgrounds I saw everywhere would stage some of the most lively and sadistic disciplinary dramas. Maybe they were historical fixtures predating modern gym equipment, evidence of some preservationist vogue,

I speculated. How quaintly antique, this old military installation, I thought, with its wood-frame barracks and coercive
Christianity!

Digging consisted of a series of exercises performed in rapid
succession to the barking rhythm of the drill instructors' whim.
"Sit-ups now!" Shouting instructions as if from the deck of a
storm-twisted ship, they'd direct this tormented pantomime
with a crazed sort of urgency. "Push-ups now!" Whereupon
the private would immediately change positions so as to exe-
cute this pressing new command. "Leg lifts now!" Another
flip. "Toe touches now!" All of it delivered with increasing
speed—a maniacal version of Simon Says. Only after a suf-
ficient amount of dirt had caked his face and his camouflage
shirt and pants were heavy with sweat would the offending
private be released.

As I say, no one in our platoon had yet experienced this
form of punishment, though we'd been doing the exercises
together, as a group, and at a mild enough pace. I must have
been the first member of that entire company to be called out
for demonstration.

We had just been issued our rifles, still clutching the paper-
work registering each serial number, as one of the island's
innumerable flies harassed my ears like an air raid siren. We
held our M16A2 rifles diagonally across our chests, at attention. My rifle sight-post near the end of the barrel was conveniently close to my face. Conveniently close to my left eye,
where the dizzy insect seemed determined to lounge in the
musk of my brow. Surreptitiously—not a popular word in the
Marine Corps—I dipped the sight-post toward the spot on my
face just then bristling with the phantom itch of fly wings.

A word of advice: when Marine Corps drill instructors tell

you to stand in formation, they don't mean stand there and chill for a bit; they expect you to stand *stock*-still, like the marines outside the White House or Air Force One—hell, like that guy covered in silver paint in Times Square who pretends he is made of aluminum.

Just then I heard my name as if it were a cheer—as if someone on the sidelines were cheering me on to a goal, like "Go, Pardlo!" Or "Yay, Pardlo!"

Suddenly, drill instructors were ringing me like white blood cells rushing a foreign body. The drill instructors overturned that calm, shiftless southern heat like a crate of oranges, their words drumming my skull, their thundering, elaborate ad hominem assessments of my masculinity, my parentage. Inches from my face. At the back of my head. Chests bumped my shoulders. Seen at a distance, if you turned the sound off, I could have been a prince being fussed over by a retinue of tailors, one of whom had just relieved me of my weapon.

Please, I thought, as they ordered me into the dirt, and my mind ratcheted like an old train station schedule board. I was afraid of the dirt. And it was—did I mention?—insanely fucking *hot.*

I undertook a very quick blame assessment. It was my father's fault. All of this. What a huge unnecessary production this had all become. What a misunderstanding. We could still fix this, couldn't we? They wanted me to say uncle? All right, then, fuck it: *uncle.* I crumpled up the weapons requisition form, like I was drying my hands with it, and dropped it right on the ground, the kind of littering I would not ordinarily do. "Listen," I said as I put my hands up, "this is all a big misunderstanding, you know? I should be home smoking a joint, sitting on my diving board. I mean, you guys, you all

take this very, very seriously. And I respect that, right? Just . . .
It's not for me."

My tormentors' barking took on a stereophonic depth, as
if they were multiplying. When I realized they had no concern
for decorum or appearances—okay, now I was getting embarrassed for them—I realized also that they wouldn't tire easily.
Nor was it like I could out-pout them. Panicking, I wept. And
continued weeping until my weeping was ontological. I didn't
give a shit what anybody thought. There was no pretense, no
masks left for me to shed.

At some point, I relented, seeing as they were going to do no
such thing. We were now standing on the edge of the pit. Duti-
fully, I climbed down into that dirt with all the showy indignation of a church matron, a vain attempt at dignity. Now I did
push-ups now in front of the entire company. I did *sit-ups now*
and knew: they were making an example of me. That's what
they were doing!—*leg lifts now!*—trained to handle the likes
of me. *Squat thrusts now!* They did not take me to be unique,
exceptional. *Jumping jacks now!* They'd seen me coming a
mile away, clearly—*Sit-ups now!*—and were not impressed.
Damn, I thought. *Mountain climbers now!* My uniform is
dirty as *fuck*.

———

There was talk of incarceration. Court-martial even. In hind-
sight, I see all of that must have been part of the drill, too, the
staging of terror and discipline. Nor was this an empty threat.
They could have been preparing to set me up with a blindfold
and cigarette against a pocked cement wall just around the
corner, for all I knew. I had committed suicide by military-

industrial complex. Surrendering all sense of reasoning, all sense of subjectivity, I turned myself into a thing. It was almost a relief except for the fact that they wouldn't allow me to sit. For what seemed like hours, I stood beside a picnic table outside the armory, looking like I had been run over by a truck, as I watched the others file past, freshly shorn and pressed, each with a greased black M16A2, haughty as Egyptian gods marching in some perfectly stylized frieze.

For the next two days while, I could only presume, the brass decided what to do with me, I was made to tag along with my platoon in a sort of limbo, following behind the formation like a POW. For hours I was made to stand off to the side while my former platoon-mates engaged in grueling training exercises on the parade deck, drilling, learning to march in formation (*eyes right!*). Finally, someone shouted for me from across the blacktop. I was told to follow this marine and report to my senior drill instructor's office. Any resolution would be blessed relief, anything that would provide some category with which to identify. "Deceased" would have worked.

For twenty minutes, I had been standing there, alone, at attention, when he arrived. He seemed almost apologetic, the senior drill instructor, when he entered the room and installed himself behind his desk, a civility of which I was immediately suspicious. That he was African American made no impression on me; I had so little understanding of U.S. military history. Between him, Sean, and the recruiting officer, I had begun to suspect that the Marine Corps, the "first to fight" in a field of battle, and thus most disposable, had been especially established for black soldiers.

My grandmother had passed away, he told me. It took me

a beat before I could translate his dialect. Tinny with a bit of banjo. "Technically," he said, "because she's not an immediate family member, you won't be given leave to attend the funeral."

Given leave? That would suggest I had some official status to be given leave *from.*

"But you do have permission to call home," he sighed as he pushed a few coins across his desk and pointed me toward a pay phone at the bottom of the stairs.

"Thank you," I managed through my unsteady face, unsure what to feel; it was the first death in the family I'd been old enough to grieve.

"Don't thank me," Sergeant Brown said. "Never thank me."

We have few rituals of passage in American culture. No secular age of accountability that hasn't been arbitrarily decided by our judicial system. No vision quests. But those first two weeks were enough to shift something fundamental in me. After the full three months of Marine Corps boot camp, I was able to recognize the difference between me and whatever besmirched thing it was that I'd made of the quilted face on the lunch truck.

In the days that followed my grandmother's passing, I was sent back to the armory without discussion to rerequisition my weapon. For the remainder of boot camp I would be given no assignments that showed me to be in the drill instructors' esteem or confidence. I was placed in no leadership roles. But I enjoyed, at least, the head-shaking deference of my peers, everyone having witnessed that rash leap into the abyss, and then my emergence therefrom, goopy and disoriented, like a newborn calf. I had become my own spirit animal. I threw myself at challenges to test my strength and ring the carnival bell of redemption. No longer did I consider digging a punishment, but rather, like some arms demonstration in the middle of the Arizona desert, an exercise in controlled fear.

Once, Sergeant Brown called me out for something incidental I no longer even remember, something small enough it gave me the sense he might have been waiting for this opportunity. Our platoon just then was camped in a forested area alongside a decommissioned airstrip. Rather than send me to the dirt, Brown ordered me into the brambles. And like Br'er Rabbit, I dove right in, shouting my assent as welts rose up on my bare forearms, histamine flooding the thorn's countless abrasions. Many years later, reading Frederick Douglass's account of his fight with Covey the slave-breaker, I recalled my contest with Brown. I was grateful to my master for staging this ritual do-over in which I might properly mourn my carefree-if-not-overprotected childhood, setting it adrift on a swift current of nostalgia.

I was only dug once or twice more after that. But, then, there was no need for it. I knew by now what was expected of me, and my bearing made it clear I considered the bargain reasonable. I was like the Ship of Theseus, replaced entirely with new parts.

Superheroes often have one-off powers that show up in particular situations—when the writers can't figure out how to resolve a conflict, for instance. Similarly, the Marine Corps endowed me with powers that I discovered in such odd circumstances that I began to wonder if they had limits at all. I couldn't do Jedi-type shit, even though once, without looking, I caught a glass that had rolled off the table. Anyway, I knew what happened to Greek heroes who started thinking they had it made. Unsure of my strength, and afraid of unforeseen consequences, I was reluctant to use even the powers I knew I

had. Afraid of myself, I self-medicated. I became my own villain. Years later, I would come to understand these superpow-
ers and the internal conflicts they precipitated, as symptoms
of bipolar disorder.

I want to go back, like some time-traveling dolphin, and
warn that young man—my eighteen-year-old self, the new
marine whose father had rented a Winnebago and driven the
family from New Jersey to South Carolina to return the prodi-
gal son home. I want to warn him of just how much he'll *need*
his powers, not for the open sea ahead, but for all the demons
lurking in the unconscious fathoms below.

So funny how I misremembered the arrangement of people in this photograph. *Left to right:* Sam Jr., Greg Sr., Sam Sr., Greg Jr. (in lap).

A mystery man who may or may not be my ancestor.

My great-grandfather Samuel Pardlo, Sr., aka "Little Bits," among the crew of riggers who helped build the USS *Wisconsin*, circa 1942.

Bob as a student at the FAA (formerly CAA) training facility, Oklahoma City, circa 1952.

Promotional photo for Greg Sr. after winning election for vice president
of the American Train Dispatchers Association, 2003.

Mom and Dad around the time of the air traffic controllers' strike.

Me, three years old.

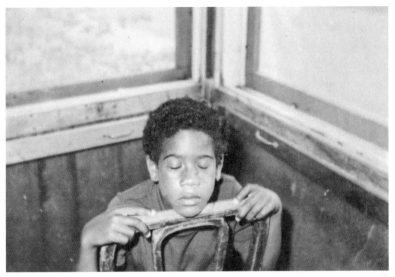

I went away to summer camp for two weeks when I was seven. I cried the first two days, but in the end I didn't want to go home.

Our neighbor Danon on the left, and me, age thirteen, holding my prized possession. Robbie is about three years old here.

We drilled for weeks preparing for graduation only to have rain force us inside to the auditorium.

My mother designed the stained-glass interior sign for the jazz club. She wanted to give it a church feel, but the neighbors asked for the windows to be boarded up and soundproofed. Even with the fluorescent light we nestled behind it in lieu of natural light, it was an iconic feature.

Celebrating Robbie after a performance by City High. *Left to right:* Michelle (my cousin), Stacia (my cousin), Robin (my aunt), Mom, Robbie, Nigel (one of my best friends from high school), Dad, me, and Donna (my aunt).

Robbie and me after my graduation (MFA in Poetry) from NYU in 2001.

Part Two

The Wreck of the Conquest

I was unconsciously reliving my father's apocalyptic crises, like they would emancipate me in a way that Marine Corps boot camp could not. The late eighties felt like a yawn of VH1 and global peace. I had been trained to lay down my life for my country, but what could it hurt if while we waited for the next conflagration I got a college degree? My immediate superior was a lance corporal who didn't appreciate that I'd enlisted to get money for college. One became a marine to fight and die, not to finance an entrée into the bourgeoisie. He made it hard for me to get information about the GI Bill, and there was no circumventing the chain of command. If information was hard to come by, getting kicked out of the Marine Corps was not. It was called an administrative separation, not quite so bad as a dishonorable discharge. Selling Yellow Pages advertising put me in a higher tax bracket than most of my fellow marines, and I resented them for not being the overachievers I wanted them to be. As I did with so many girlfriends, I sabotaged my relationship with the Marine Corps. We parted ways after two years of the six I was contracted for. Like the girlfriends, they were happy to see me go.

My mother, meanwhile, had risen to an executive position at the Yellow Pages. She supervised thirty-three artists in eleven offices across the state of Pennsylvania. I got a job in the mailroom at the office where she worked. The sales teams there generated most of the interoffice correspondence that kept me busy throughout the day, and I got to know them very well as a result. I wanted to be one of them. The first time I interviewed for a sales position, no one took me seriously. I was just a plucky kid. The second time I interviewed, I was hopped-up on Zig Ziglar and Dale Carnegie. They gave me a position in telephone sales. On the phone, I could assume a level of frankness with my customers. Our interactions weren't distorted by the interference of race. The phone was like a superhero's mask, and I found it very easy to sell advertising. Many of my coworkers raised families and put their kids through college with the kind of commissions I pulled in. I lived with my parents. Partying didn't relieve the financial swell fast enough, so I traded in my Pontiac Fiero for a Chrysler Conquest I picked up at one of those "Everyone Is Approved!" dealerships on Route 38.

I had the car for three months. Driving home from the bars at night, I took back roads and liked to floor it along one particular stretch beside a cornfield. One evening, I lost control and launched the Conquest into the rows of stubble. The police officer who fished me out of the steaming junk could see that I was shitfaced, but figured I had enough problems with the car and didn't bust me for drunk driving. I took a few days off from work to figure things out, and only went back in to tell my manager that I quit. It was an impulsive move, one I regretted when, after insurance covered the Kelley Blue Book value of the car, I was on the hook for an eight-thousand-dollar balance. It wasn't fair that I should continue to pay three hundred dollars a month for the useless leather and steel heaped at the curb in front of my house like abstract art. I ran from the debt for nearly twenty years until a collection agency found me in Brooklyn and seized my (and my new wife's) bank accounts.

Someone told me that I was old enough to apply for guaranteed student loans on my own without my parents' cosignature. I hadn't saved any money, and with neither the GI Bill nor a serviceable credit score, I proudly planted my first sapling of college loan debt that would one day top out near two hundred grand. "Lifelong learner" was an attractive mantle for a number of reasons. It was my right as a citizen. Also, the debt stayed in deferment as long as I was in school. It was a mind game anyway. Debt was about as real as race, meaning not real at all, but capable of fucking up my life in lasting ways.

I met Maya, who would become my first wife, in 1990, after completing my first year back in school at Rutgers. Half Danish, she was visiting her father's side of the family in New Jersey for the summer. We met through friends. Maya worked in a bookstore. She brought books home to her aunt's house in a Trenton suburb, where we smoked cigarettes and read together beside the pool. By August, Maya was bored with suburban America, ready to go back home. I had plans to follow her to a country that weeks earlier I couldn't have located on a map. As always (post–boot camp), I did my homework. Copenhagen had attracted black artists, musicians, and writers like Walter Henry Williams, Don Cherry, William H. Johnson, and Nella Larsen. Paris was a cliché. Copenhagen was my calling, and a hipper Promised Land than Paris for black intellectuals escaping the stifling air pollution of American racism. That fall I prepared to spend my spring semester abroad, studying at the University of Copenhagen.

I landed in Copenhagen on Christmas Day, and was promptly detained at the airport. Customs officials were suspicious of me because I had a one-way ticket and four hundred dollars in traveler's checks in my fanny pack. They made me show them the traveler's checks. I spread them out on the stainless-steel table in the customs office. Stiffer than cash, the checks reminded me of the Treasury bills my parents had saved for me before the strike. My mother and I had laid them out on the kitchen table to admire. That one visual confirmation of my future was enough to convince me that college was my fate. I never saw the T-bills again, but they were with me in spirit, a self-fulfilling promise of class mobility. Broke as hell, hair in some funky-ass braids, I sat alone in the office waiting for Maya's father, Tom, to come claim me, all the while feeling my blue passport entitled me to be and go wherever I chose in the world.

On his own, Tom raised Maya and Jamie, her brother. But by the time I arrived, Tom lived alone in the four-bedroom flat he owned on the top floor of a converted seventeenth-century army barracks. A self-taught linguist, Tom had made a career teaching Danish to English speakers. I saw familiar authoritarian tendencies in Tom, but unlike my father, Tom enjoyed my eagerness to please him. He was my language tutor. I was his star pupil.

During my second week of classes at the University of Copenhagen, a professor approached me to express his wonder at how fate had delivered me to his seminar. This course, the History of Law in Western Europe, was conducted in English, and it attracted a cosmopolitan cohort, including a black Brit from Oxford; the professor's fascination with me wasn't racially motivated. That I was from, as I told everyone, a public university in New Jersey seemed more remarkable to him than my blackness. I understood even then that the professor's wonder was benign—perhaps a little congratulatory. But the message I took away was that I was fantastically out of my league. "Fate," to use his word, politely led me to the door and excused me from ever having to return to that school, an excuse that allowed me to spend more time with Maya.

My first job after dropping out of the university was delivering newspapers. It made practical use of my military training. I humped Sunday editions of *Berlingske Tidende* up six and seven flights of stairs, across neighborhoods I knew only from the hand-drawn maps I was given at the distribution garage. I would rest occasionally and study the newspapers to improve my vocabulary and to record phrases and idioms I would ask Tom to explain later. Tom liberated me from my monolingual pigeonhole.

The youngest of four, Tom grew up in an upper-middle-class family from West Chester, Pennsylvania. His father had owned a chain of grocery stores successful enough to seed the family's financial security for several generations. Their liberal bona fides were proved by their disregard for the fact that I was black. Tom had landed in Copenhagen after leaving West Chester to evade the draft during the war in Vietnam. He graduated high school, and his father gave him a roll of cash, sending him north to Canada. Tom's travels then took him to Europe and North Africa, until he met Maya's mom, a Danish woman, and they made a home in her native land of socialism and pickled herring.

Far from my original plan to spend no more than a semester abroad at the University of Copenhagen, I began to imagine

my life among the hippie socialists, the children Maya and I
might have: umber-afro'ed Vikings I'd wheel around the gentrifying neighborhood of Christianshavn in my cargo bike. I
would master Danish, among other European languages, naturally. Maya and I would debate global politics with polyglot
friends and neighbors during frequent dinner parties that we
would host in the courtyard behind our canal-view apartment.
Summer vacations we would spend in a cabin at the beach,
where I imagined our kids flinging themselves against the
sharp, frigid waves. It didn't hurt that, once married, I would
be eligible for state welfare, health care, and job training; and,
most important, I could go back to the university for free. We
were married in April 1991, in Copenhagen's city hall.

———

Unfortunately, Maya got bored again. Copenhagen wasn't as
romantic for her as it was for me. We had gotten the news that
my grandfather Bob had bought a little neighborhood bar in
Merchantville, New Jersey, and that together the family had
turned it into a jazz club. Maya suggested we move back to the
States to help out. Still, I had decided I wanted to be a writer,
and nurturing that vision of myself required keeping a safe distance from my family.

Before I flew to Copenhagen in 1990, my aunt Donna gave
me a copy of Richard Wright's *The Outsider*. Critics considered *The Outsider* a failed novel, but I didn't need the protagonist, Cross Damon, to be anything more than a mouthpiece
for Wright's ideological rants. I was still terrified of the goopy
provincialism and social barriers that trapped people forever
in small towns like mine. Cross, a suicidal alcoholic adulterer,
amateur intellectual, and writer, articulated ambitions and

anxieties I hadn't yet figured out how to frame. Cross worked at the post office, and survived a tragic subway derailment on his way to work one day. When police misidentified one of the many casualties in the train crash as Cross, he retreated into the shadows, and let everyone—his job, family, and friends— believe he was dead. Cross became "a man standing outside of the world." The book entered my imagination like a horoscope. I'd survived a series of metaphorical wrecks, but I read Cross's subway derailment as analogous to the one literal wreck that had cost me my credit score.

Now back in the United States, I was reminded how much the lack of credit limited my freedom. My student loans came crawling out of deferment. I took on two and three jobs at a time, and vowed that I would register for classes as soon as we had stable finances. It was an empty promise.

The Serengeti Café & Jazz Club got a lot of buzz when it opened. My mother handled the marketing and décor. My aunt Robin, my mother's youngest sister, took care of accounting, inventory, and other administrative responsibilities. My father got a certificate in mixology and tended bar for tips. He worked only Friday and Saturday nights, when marquee bands attracted upscale crowds, and taught me how to bar-back so I could fill in whenever he decided a customer didn't merit the privilege of his attention. Maya and I helped wait tables on the weekends.

Bert, a local who had managed the place for the previous owner, was a convenient buffer, able to placate the old shot-and-beer crowd until we could afford to price them out and cater exclusively to high-end customers. Bert didn't get that his days were numbered, but I did. After a year of riding buses and bicycles to work fourteen-hour days at my various weekday jobs, I let go of my dream of being a writer and told Bob it was time for Bert to go. I wanted his job. In lieu of a salary, Bob agreed to cover all my bills and expenses so Maya and I could run the business free from the distraction of debts. The bar had once been a speakeasy attached to a large house. The rest of the building was vacant and habitable. Maya and I moved into the apartment over the bar to save on rent.

I would have been a decent bar manager if I didn't have to work in the bar, too. Some customers worried about my drinking, but because the crowd rotated, I could pass off each drunk spell as an isolated binge, a bad night. Friends and regular customers who were around often enough to have seen the "Greg falls off the bar stool" or the "Greg is hitting on someone's girlfriend" episodes multiple times expressed concern. Otherwise, the business thrived for the better part of a decade.

Maya eventually left me in search of a less destructive lifestyle, and my partying got worse. Bob fired me regularly, for my own good, but while I lived upstairs, I had nowhere else to go. I thought it was time to try school again, and because I hadn't had any real income in four years, I was eligible for a Pell Grant, which would cover most of my tuition. I had befriended a law student, Chad, who hung out at the club. He and I sat up long nights talking and arguing about books. When one of his roommates moved out, he offered me the spot in the house he was sharing with a bunch of guys, recent grads who had all been English majors at Rutgers. I took out additional student loans to cover my rent and moved in. It was not far from the club and a twenty-minute bike ride from campus. Stringing together enough sober days in a row, I convinced myself that I wasn't an alcoholic after all. I made dean's list my first semester back. I tended bar on occasion, but I didn't have to, because

I'd maxed out what I could borrow each semester in student loans. As much as any rich kid, I deserved to go through college carefree. It was a Faustian luxury, but one I accepted. By the time I graduated in the late nineties, I would stop by the club out of familial duty, the way one visits grandparents.

We knew most of our customers well, and tried to accommodate them with whatever form of credit we could extend when they needed it. A reckless, enabling generosity for sure. A binder under the bar bulged with unpaid tabs, accounts receivable on hand-scribbled guest checks. It was that kind of place. One night, not long after I had moved to New York for grad school, one of the regulars, I was told, stopped in for a drink and realized she was out of cash. She offered to pay with a personal check. I picture the bartender that night waving her off, saying *next time,* and I picture her insisting. Some days later, Bob found out that the young professional woman had been barhopping all night since happy hour, and never made it home. She drove her car into a tree and died. I think of Daphne, who escaped Apollo by turning into a tree. Apollo memorialized her by wearing a branch of her leaves on his head. Because the only paper trail, the check, led to Serengeti and nowhere else, the woman's family sued the club for continuing to serve her when she must have been visibly intoxicated. Bob lost everything in the lawsuit, every asset belonging to Dad N' Girls, Inc., the company he'd formed to own and operate the club. What survives of the family business? Shared memories, a few "Best of South Jersey" plaques, a generation of suburbanites like myself, who, without Serengeti, might never have grown to appreciate music as an audience-inclusive, communal undertaking. This, then, is my inheritance, my jazz trust, a mythos in sheet music and tablature. Her life for a wreath of laurels.

He Ain't Heavy

I n addition to my brother, Robbie, the R&B trio City High
included Ryan and Claudette. All three had attended Willingboro High School, like I did. A year after he graduated,
Robbie signed with Booga Basement Records, a recording
company that grew out of a small studio in South Orange, New
Jersey, where the Fugees recorded *The Score*. Claudette was
Robbie's girlfriend at the time. She was two grades behind him
and had not yet graduated. She was pretty and racially ambiguous, and, much to everyone's surprise, she could carry a tune.
The two added Ryan Toby, who had already achieved some
notoriety as the kid who sang "Oh, Happy Day" with Whoopi
Goldberg in *Sister Act* 2. For whatever reason—jealousy,
youth, hubris—City High never jelled. They remained as disinterested in one another's careers as commuters carpooling to
a common office park.

Robbie took it personally. He was profligate and reaction-
ary. With money, he had the discretion of a leaf blower. He
bought expensive clothes for people he hardly knew, clothes
for himself. Like some lotto-opulent hoarder, he let the clothes

heap up; mounds of them lay on his bedroom floor in the house he still shared with our parents. So many nauseating emblems of the skin he couldn't shed fast enough. City High broke up in 2002. Within five years, my brother burned through more than a million dollars in W-2 income. Who knows how much he made from studio work, endorsements, and other side hustles? My mother pinched the occasional royalty check and invested it for him. She was reluctant to do more than that. So many unscrupulous mothers of famous children muddy the line between care and grand larceny.

From my vantage, City High's success looked so carefree that I thought Robbie was contriving petty dramas with Claudette, Ryan, and the ensemble of women he paraded through my parents' house. *That's how it started,* I thought at the time; *he got lost in a self-made labyrinth again and again as a cry for attention. All that operatic weeping and screaming, and storming into the night to make people worry about him.* I'm sorry I didn't take it seriously until 2009, when we were all forced onto the stage of his commedia dell'arte.

My brother dismantled his music career in a series of alternating excesses dropping like feet in an iambic line: blackouts and shape-shifting rage. No one in the industry would risk working with him. City High had released a Grammy-nominated album, but they were not yet enough of a commodity for people to suffer Robbie's inebriated, uncooperative, and belligerent company. A manic-depressive, he had been born to heartbreak, and alcohol provided a reason for the hurt that he couldn't locate or conquer. "I like the not-giving-a-fuck" you get from being drunk, he'd later tell television cameras on A&E's *Intervention.*

My mother had worried that we wouldn't bond and that Robbie would languish in the long shadow I cast across the decade that separated us. Per her instructions, I'd pack him and his snack bag into his stroller and push my toddler brother around the neighborhood to wherever my friends were hanging out. I was thirteen, and my radius was defined by my access to the bathrooms of friendly neighbors. I had established a network of safe houses I could get Robbie to in an emergency. Some neighbors called me "Gweg-Gweg," which they'd heard Robbie yell from behind a bathroom door when he needed me to come and help him wipe.

Robbie was my sidekick then, and he was my father's, too. Greg Sr. called Robbie "Babakazoo," after a character in the movie *Thank God It's Friday*. Whenever he was feeling nostalgic, Big Greg reminded us that he used to load Robbie into the car and set out with a single objective: to explore strange new worlds. To hear them tell it, their adventures were quixotic and epic. "What are we going to do today, Babakazoo?" my father would ask excitedly. With a tagline worthy of a child star, Robbie would reply, "Dad, we're gunna *go* and *see*!"

He was precocious in some ways, but Robbie proved less resourceful in school than I had been. My mother hired tutors. Looking for ways to build his self-esteem, she'd signed him up for PAL football. Robbie's behavior grew increasingly erratic. My mother's concerns escalated from yellow alert to red. She boasted of a new drug, Ritalin, that she hoped would be Robbie's minder when none of us were around.

She protected him from impatient teachers and dodged

administrators who recommended remedial classes with extra-curricular detentions and suspensions. She hustled Robbie through an assortment of public and Catholic schools in our suburban South Jersey, which meant she often had to orga-nize her life around dropping him off and picking him up. My mother knew that, unprotected, black boys could get lost like a marble in the Rube Goldberg machine of public education, only to be quietly collected in the eager baskets of the criminal justice system.

Contrary to what my father believed, my mother was the brains of the family. People said she looked like Tina Turner. A laughable observation, it referred mostly to their similar skin tone. My mom did want our house to be full of music and art like the house she grew up in—minus the drunk drama. Before Robbie was born, she hired a piano teacher to come to our house once a week. Big Greg had never played an instrument, and he encouraged me to keep up with my lessons because he'd watched a boy once capture everyone's attention at a house party by poking at a few keys. "He stole my thunder," said my father, for whom going to a party was a competition he could lose only to someone who was aided by a prop. I hated practic-ing. I abandoned the piano, but before my voice changed, I had an admirable run in the All South Jersey Choir.

When my parents discovered that Robbie could really sing, they popped champagne bottles like ballplayers in a locker room. "He hit that note," my father drawled whenever he told the story about Robbie's maiden performance at a middle school talent show, "and grown women were falling out in the aisles!" My father measured success in art by the degrees of female enchantment and male envy it inspired, but maternal pragmatism guided Robbie to heights. My mom determined that music would protect his institutionally endangered life. It began as a rescue operation but settled into martial law.

My mother allowed Robbie to go to our town's public high school for his junior and senior years only because it boasted a celebrated music program. By the time he graduated in 1997, my brother had participated in summer programs at Freedom Theatre in Philadelphia and Berklee College of Music in Boston. Dispatches from Robbie's life in the music industry reached me like gossip and inspired envy. In 1998, I was a thirty-year-old junior in college. My little brother who was not even old enough to drink was singing backup vocals on Whitney Houston's "My Love Is Your Love." My little brother was voice-training with Teddy Pendergrass. He also had a cut on the soundtrack for the movie *Life,* starring Eddie Murphy and Martin Lawrence. The song that appeared on that soundtrack, "What Would You Do?," was credited to his fledgling group.

———

Some pop music fans misinterpreted City High's hit song, "What Would You Do?," as social critique. Listeners mistook the song's moralizing respectability politics for affirmation meant to empower a stereotypically young, financially insecure single mother trying to provide for herself and her child. Slut-shaming was seen as a pep talk. The music video begins with my brother and his bandmates, Ryan and Claudette, sitting on the stoop of a brownstone in Brooklyn. "Bottom line, Lonnie's a ho, yo. She's a ho," says Robbie in the opening segment.

"What Would You Do?" is the account of a young man, a

few years out of high school. He goes to a party and unexpectedly runs into a former classmate. Her name is Lonnie. Lonnie is among the "five or six strippers tryna work for a buck." In the music video, there are two women. One wears a red-and-black negligee. The white feathered negligee belongs to Lonnie, I'm sure, who ditches it as she dances for the men. Then Lonnie lifts her matching white bikini top over her head, and pixels bloom to cover her breasts, either to protect her modesty from my gaze or to protect me from her immodesty, while the men in the video stand shoulder to shoulder, watching. The women could be roosters slashing each other with lethal talons. Some of the men sway tensely like straphangers on a subway. Others throw bills and wag wads of cash in time with the music.

Robbie told me a bachelor party inspired the song, although the video depicted a gathering somewhat more debauched for its lack of a discernible purpose. I felt complicit. I couldn't be a disinterested onlooker. The camera made me aware of my masculinity, and ashamed. I was one of these men. I was in my kitchen, scrubbing the video back and forth, as if to shake my head no and to say, "I don't belong here, I am better than them."

I'd wondered about Robbie's motives. Pop Star Robbie singles "Lonnie" out of the crowd and leads her away from where she was earning money to the rooftop. There, in private, he intervenes and attempts to rescue her, convinced his intrusion is necessary and gallant. He urges her to find a respectable way to provide for her fatherless son. Her appeals, protests, and recrimination are no match for his disapproval and Freudian logic: "If my mother could do it" (is he implicating *my* mother?), could raise a fatherless child without banking on the wages of erotic dancing, then "baby you can do it." The question I couldn't ask Robbie because it would uncork a miasma of misogynistic fears was why should it be any of his fucking business.

For the record, I was not at the bachelor party; nor was I in the video. I was interviewing Robbie for this book, and he was on the phone with me. I was reminding him—an entirely rhetorical extravagance on my part—that we grew up with our father. I wanted to figure out where he'd gotten these ideas from. "Our family couldn't have been any more nuclear! A picket fence, for chrissakes. Ozzie and fucking Harriet. Maybe you felt guilty," I said.

"That's one way to think about it," is all he would say. Still, I wanted to know, if he was so damned invested in Lonnie's well-being, why didn't he offer to babysit or go grocery shopping for her? Why couldn't he offer his support instead of condemning her? Before we ended our phone call, I asked him how he might want to be remembered after he was dead. I was thinking about our father. I wanted to believe that we can change our behavior, that we are not the behaviors that we inherit. "What do you want people to say about you when you're gone?" I asked my brother.

I am biased, but I don't think it is only my bias speaking when I say that Robbie was the most talented member of City High. He was also the most dysfunctional. Maybe he had wanted success to transform him into someone else. When he saw that success hadn't turned him into an idealized version of himself, he pushed success aside like a plate of vegetables he refused to eat. "They should say that I brought music into the lives of people all around the world," he answered. "That

I was able to lighten someone's sadness, lift someone's weight with my songs." I wanted to point out that this is what people could already say about him. I wanted to think my brother was happy, that he achieved all he wanted at a tender age. I didn't want to believe that at thirty-seven, as I was writing this book, Robbie already thought of his life in the past tense. I wanted to believe we both had many more places to go and see.

"Hurrah for Schoelcher!"

She was remarkably agile with her orgasms, my interim girl-friend between marriages, and could match mine at will. It was fun until it wasn't anymore. At least it wasn't enough, not for her, and she started bullying me into a new game: searching deep in each other's eyes as we climaxed together. We watched ourselves fucking in the closet's mirrored doors—the yin and yang we made with our interracial bodies—the mirror filtering our material presence to let the two-dimensional spectacle of us flicker, free of intention, a fun-house diversion. It was a buffer; the mirror gave me space to mull and muse. This new project, though, seemed strange—the whole vis-à-vis of it. By demanding my eyes she divided me from myself. At first, I thought it was corny, if not even a bit Bela Lugosi. But after some time—I mean, really, what choice did I have? I threw myself into it.

———

"Vagal tone," which is not a tone at all, says something about one's capacity for personal interaction and, according to at least one website, an "ability to tune in to the frequency of the human voice." The ability to make and hold eye contact, as well as having the ear for subtle fluctuations in attitude: these are the essence of sociability and healthy relationships—the groundwork for getting along. "Vague," from the root "vagus," is also the name of the nerve that serves the lungs and stomach, the nerve likely responsible for our gut responses to stimuli. But there is something about the vagal tone that approved science doesn't capture. Something analogous to the functioning of star signs and mood rings. "I don't like your tone," we hear, reminding us that mothers can decrypt the truth-frequencies buried in our hearts.

"Fuera de onda," my mother-in-law tells me in her hippie slang when I'm having a bad Spanish day. It's not that I don't know the basic grammar or that my limited vocabulary excludes me from certain dinner table conversations, but that I'm just *tuned out* on those occasions, that I can't (or won't) pick up the wavelength that bonds the dining family in common understanding.

Unaligned or inharmonious vagal tones can fuck up interactions in my own language, too. Like when I find myself staring dumbly, trying to decipher the banal quip of a fellow straphanger in my subway car. Sometimes I fail to pick up the rhythms of the voice on the page I'm reading. If, for example, I'm reading an essay or article with an unfamiliar byline, I might have difficulty making sense of the sentences until I see a word with a British spelling. Suddenly the whole becomes intelligible because I've begun unconsciously assigning a British accent to my subvocalization of the text.

I've even experienced this sort of estrangement in silence, sharing an elevator, pretending not to notice a stranger, refusing her the simple grace of recognition, while trying to think up a comment whimsical and seemingly spontaneous enough to suggest I had only just noticed she was even standing there. It's often in moments like these that I fear the power of eye contact the most.

———

A stereotype is a kind of veil. The sculpture of Booker T. Washington at Tuskegee University, as I recall, depicts him lifting the veil of ignorance from a half-naked former bondsman, newly emancipated and crouched on top of a plow and an anvil. I've never been able to figure out why the former slave is hunched up under this heavy cloth in the first place, considering this is Alabama. When Ellison's Invisible Man encounters this famous statue, he finds it puzzling, too. He can't decide, he says, "whether the veil is really being lifted, or lowered more firmly into place; whether I am witnessing a revelation or a more efficient blinding." The former slave has a book in his lap, which suggests Washington may be exposing the man's covert (and in fact criminal) literacy. Maybe it's a fetal position the man is in and he's not really a former slave at all, but only a symbol of Washington's own homuncular former self? His id, maybe? What if Washington lifts the veil of oppressive social norms in order to emancipate himself as an individual? It's maddening that the sculpture resists our knowing. This reminds me of Rilke's line "We cannot know his legendary head . . ."

While many of us decry those veils of identity we call stereotypes, especially when they're projected onto us, some others of us embrace stereotypes. Embracing them can be comforting, a way of announcing we belong *somewhere*, if not, perhaps, here. Defending his right to populate his poems unapologetically with images he considers "true" regardless of whether or not they are stereotypical, a promising young poet said to me once, "But I *do* like fried chicken!" Yes, I said, and I like white women. But these are clichés no matter the hateful inferences they bear and so the rootstock of monster-making. He means he wants to express his cultural conditioning without shame or apology, I know, which is as admirable as it is naive.

Shame is healthy. It keeps us from doing dumb shit. I would not put fried chicken in a poem just to thumb my nose at decorum. Nor would I espouse a taste for white women in a poem unless the point was to trouble the cultural foundations on which that ideological house is built. What's shameful is when poets, writers, artists deny culpability for perpetuating stereotypes or, worse yet, when we champion stereotypes to pander to our readers' need to believe in a predictable, knowable world.

———

The vagus nerve, which is the tenth cranial nerve, also regulates the autonomic activity of the bowels and the heart. The aggregated rhythm of this orchestra of flex is called the "vagal tone." I think of this as an actual tone, a Pavlovian note or a musical figure forming a chord like the love-cry of God: *Aum*. But no. Tonal frequency might be a useful metaphor, but here "tone" means something like "disposition." Empathy is an involuntarily harmonic response to the tonal emanations of others, and vagal misalignment is, perhaps literally, plucked nerves.

———

The Orgasm Queen and I met as nontraditional undergrads— both of us in our mid-twenties—returning to college with a righteous hunger for lost time, and little patience for sentimental attachments. She discovered Freud and explained, despite my wincing protests, how she based the O-face game on that reading. It was a little fascinating, but mostly cruel, to focus entirely on each other, provoking our own self-consciousness and forcing each other to confront our own vulnerability.

I looked through Freud's writing on sexuality. This might have been a mistake. I took away cynicism that he probably didn't intend. I deduced that men may be incapable of experiencing both empathy and desire at once. The incest taboo serves as a kind of mental epiglottis, preventing one function from interfering with the other. Male empathy is reserved for the saintly or the maternal, and the incest taboo prevents sexual feelings for anyone associated with either of those categories. Empathic identification, then, I believed was a categorical obstacle to the sexual appetite, an anorectic, something that had to be cleared away to make room for desire.

This train of thought ran off the rails almost as soon as it left the station. I knew it wouldn't take me anywhere a morally responsible person could want to go. Still, gluttonous, I kept reading. Was the Orgasm Queen's objective in the O-face game to liberate me from a puddle of lust, and to release me into the oceanic currents of mature human attachment? Paranoia got the better of me. I succumbed to the suspicion that she was less concerned with my emotional growth than with her own fear that I might be secretly debasing her during sex. She couldn't accept the idea that sexual encounters might entail some imbalance of power. To prevent either one of us from being the Thesis, she would ensure we were both Antitheses, locked in contrast with each other. My attention would have to be driven away from my body, away from my masculinity—

which amounted, and I know this is a stretch, to a kind of castration. Figuratively speaking. How else could we level the field?

When I factored in my hang-ups with race, things got a little problematic. Perhaps our racial difference prompted her to fixate on the conventionally gendered power dynamics in our sexual relationship. Was it my phallus she wanted to neutralize or, more specifically, my *black* phallus? After all, I had no way of telling what she was like in bed with non-black dudes or with women. Nor was I about to make what I am sure she would have considered a repugnant proposition in order to find out.

More likely is that the O-face game was just that, a game. Why couldn't I be cool with that? Wherefore these fears of castration? Maybe they were a projection of guilt, an unconscious belief that I'd done something for which I *needed* to atone, to surrender my humble pound of flesh? How the hell did I get so fucked-up?

The philosopher Emmanuel Levinas believes the face-to-face encounter is the foundation of ethics. According to Levinas, the divine is a by-product of this type of encounter, which transcends either individual's desires and insecurities. But I'll be honest, I've never seen it. The closest to transcendence I ever felt in that O-face game of my sexual youth was something approximating, you know, pee-shyness. The experience however was *arresting*. So overwhelmed was I by being seen that I could no longer take pleasure in looking. When I did look, I found myself rummaging for signs of betrayal. I looked for insincerity and opportunism, and I let my paranoia play itself out until I saw only the craven nightmare of a black ram tupping a white ewe reflected in her blue eyes.

Eventually the racial fantasy subsided and I found, if not confidence, then at least absence of fear enough to stand in the void, and when I was able to do so, that vulnerability, that boundless intimacy, made me giddy. A smile would buck into a snort and together we'd be rolling off the bed in fits of flush-faced laughter. Sometimes my gaze bled into true longing, as if she were the beloved from a past life come to sit with me awhile.

———

The poet Sterling Brown numbers seven racial stereotypes "considered important enough for separate classification . . . : (1) The Contented Slave; (2) The Wretched Freeman; (3) The Comic Negro; (4) The Brute Negro; (5) The Tragic Mulatto; (6) The Local Color Negro; and (7) The Exotic Primitive." Some of these are dated and since Brown's writing in 1933 have passed out of the popular imagination. But numbers 3, 4, 6, and 7, would you please step forward and repeat the line "Ayo, ah fux wit dat on da rill, nahmean?" The twenty-first-century dialect of Ghostface Killah sounds as natural in these stereotypes' mouths as would that of their contemporary Jess B. Semple, Langston Hughes's fictional urban mouthpiece. Is this because we lack the imagination to produce new stereotypes? Or is this, as I suspect, a case of life imitating art, the cultural tropism of consensual truth? These stereotypes persist because they are culturally expedient. They do a lot of work for us, no matter where we stand with them.

One species of stereotype distinguished by Spike Lee, in an interview at Yale University in 2001, purports to be relatively mint: the Magical Negro. That character's sole function is to be support staff to the virile protagonist in the Hollywood narrative. We've known this character for ages. In love, the Magical Negro is the hip Cyrano who stays in the shadows or waits at the other end of the bar in the nightclub, texting wildly inventive pickup lines to his boy who is trying to score. In battle, he is a sycophantic Patroclus, throwing his body in harm's way. In training, no matter the discipline, he is Yoda (or Mr. Miyagi—obviously, the term "Magical Negro" is open and affirming). In times of moral dilemma, he is Huck's buddy Jim. In short, the Magical Negro is the asexual mentor or sidekick who sacrifices his own experience of life in order to instruct his young master.

The stereotype of the Magical Negro stands like the muddy Mississippi between African American men, particularly fathers and sons. It is a divisive paradigm because, having been forced to play supporting roles in public life for generations, a brother can be forgiven for being doubly protective of his own sense of agency at home. There is the presumption that a finite amount of agency is allotted each black man in the world, and that agency must be jealously maintained by exercising it whenever possible. It's tough, then, to construct a black masculine identity that is generous and self-effacing without seeming weak or auxiliary. It is almost a cultural imperative that black men be alpha males, that we construct ourselves as the dominant centers of our respective spheres; else we place our black authenticity at risk. "I'm a grown-ass man," we bark at disinterested passersby.

Around the same time that Sterling Brown published his seven stereotypes, Vladimir Propp published his *Morphology of the Folktale*. Although the *Morphology* wasn't available in English until 1958, and neither was Brown's system available in Russian, Propp likewise identifies seven folk characters:

(1) the villain; (2) the dispatcher who divulges the problem or "lack" and sends the hero off; (3) the magical helper who aids the hero in his or her quest; (4) the princess (or prize); (5) the donor who gives the hero a magical object; (6) the hero; and (7) the *false* hero who "takes credit for the hero's actions or tries to marry the princess." I'm fascinated with this taxonomy because of how easily it maps onto what I think is a sterotypical narrative of African American masculinity perpetuated in popular culture. In the life of (6) the Hero, i.e., any black man, if (1) the Villain isn't a wholly undifferentiated abstraction like "The Man," the Villain is most often some agent of institutionalized racism—a teacher, cop, or employer, for example. (2) The Dispatcher would be a galvanizing figure, like a grandmother or a single mom. Unlike the Magical Negro, (3) the Magical Helper is rarely an older, mentoring male figure for the black male hero. More often the Magical Helper is a younger sibling or relative or lifelong friend. (5) The Donor might be a music producer or an athletic talent scout, and (7) the False Hero is the bearer of an indistinct and unresolved beef that often bears homoerotic overtones. We shouldn't mistake the "ride-or-die" female companion for (4) the Princess, because by definition one doesn't compete for the devotion of a ride-or-die girl. The Princess/Prize must be perennially unattainable, for once she is attained, the story ends. It occurs to me now that I may just be describing the plot to *Breakin' 2: Electric Boogaloo.*

I tried to convince myself that simultaneous orgasms arrived at so easily were proof that the two of us were well-matched lovers, the unparalleled Leo-Sagitarius merger. Every now and then, though, when I wanted to have a selfish moment I found it was virtually impossible; it was virtually impossible, I mean, for us *not* to come at the same time. I don't know if she ever tried to go it alone, but whenever my body began to lock on target or felt hers doing it, our rhythms would synch up, and I'd be pulled into that cosmic event. There was no eating alone in bed. Neither of us could hide a cookie from the other. Like it or not, we had to share.

———

According to their publicists, Marina Abramović and Ulay broke up because they felt they were stagnating as artists and collaborators, that their creative arc had run its course. It was never entirely clear why this meant they had to end their romantic relationship. I did not give the question much thought. Somewhere in the roped-off catacombs of my mind lies a belief that great art requires great sacrifice, and a hope that there are artists presently on earth capable of making such sacrifices. But then I learned Abramović's decision to break up with Ulay ain't have shit to do with art. Ulay had just knocked up their translator, and so Abramović dumped him and didn't speak to him for decades—after they'd staged an epic breakup performance piece for the BBC, that is, in which Ulay set off from the westernmost end of the Great Wall of China, in the Gobi Desert, and Abramović from the easternmost end, near the Yellow Sea. They walked for ninety days, nonstop, until they met to say goodbye, embraced one last time, and continued on, their backs to each other now, to complete their separate remaining lengths of the wall, some fifteen hundred miles altogether, a kind of cooling-off period, as their shadows lengthened in the evening sun, with neither of them even once looking back.

Scrub forward to Abramović's show at MoMA in 2010, *The Artist Is Present,* and it seems almost as if the whole drama of their love has been staged for this climactic reunion. All tension is good tension. For this retrospective, the artist sat for 736.5 consecutive hours, not counting when the museum was closed—the equivalent of an entire month of ten-hour workdays—during which she invited people to sit down across from her for staring contests: staring contests that she always won. Museumgoers were allowed to sit for as long as they wanted to, as long as they could, gazing into the abyss of the seer's impassive face. Most people ended up weeping. Some found God. Those museumgoers formed a support group on Facebook.

This was cake, of course, compared with some of Abramović's earlier stunts. She once stood for hours and let people do whatever they wanted to with her body using a range of props from a table nearby. The table held "a gun, a bullet, a whip, lipstick, a scalpel, a coat, shoes, and olive oil." It was performance enough, that well-provisioned table, whether she was there or not. Did it make her happy to confront the fact of her vulnerability? Or was she simply proving that she was the ultimate tough girl, able to withstand anything a mortal might wield against her?

But could she withstand love? When Ulay showed up at MoMA all those years later, they didn't make him stand in line, hour after desperate hour, like all the other thousands of hopeful souls, but ushered him right into the great room where the oracle sat. The money shot is that moment of mutual recognition, when after so many hours of devotees crumpling under the pressure of Marina's soulful gravity, the one person who has not only passed within her orbit and maintained his own, but actually tugged hers slightly into variance, into a wobble, sits before her now to disrupt all space and time. I could not watch the footage of that event without feeling ashamed for the paucity of love I have allowed in my life. I wept, too.

———

I'm reminded of the Orgasm Queen whenever I think of Lacan's mirror stage—the moment when the infant recognizes its face in the mirror and realizes something has gone terribly wrong. Until that point, the infant believes she is in union with all consciousness. The poet and literary critic Fred Moten speculates toward a racialized mirror stage, which I find echoed in the cultural prohibition against "reckless eyeballing"—that is to say, a black male of sexual maturity gazing at a white woman in a way that may be construed as desirous—the very fictitious, it turns out, infraction for which Emmet Till, among so many others, was murdered. Historically, the desiring gaze of the black male has been subject to mortal repercussions, resulting in a disablement black males may internalize along with their acquisition of other basic cultural norms (a distrust of police, for example, and the internalized logic of bureaucracy). Some of us just don't look. Some of us do look, and feel ashamed for doing so. Some of us overcompensate by making a show of looking at all manner of women indiscriminately, all the while announcing this to be an expression of sexual prerogative, daring anyone to object. Admirable are those black men who fall nowhere along this spectrum of pathology.

It is within the field of my lover's fantasy of me, I suppose, that I feel most desirable. But I can't know that fantasy; I can only know my own projection of what I think that fantasy might look like, or what I might wish it to look like. I beg my lover's reciprocal objectification, fueled by the fetish value of race. In this sense, I employ racist stereotypes of black male sexual prowess in order to facilitate my own climax. It is protective. That stereotype is like a modesty sheet I drape between my white lover and me.

———

I don't care to be considered American to the exclusion of my *African* Americanness. I don't want to be considered post-black or ex-colored. If I was raised black for the most part, it was for economic reasons and apathy. Growing up, my family was not observant, preferring instead to derive our esprit de corps from the community of consumers we'd gather in fellow-ship with in the tabernacle of Macy's, the mead hall of IKEA. I am not, in other words, a Practicing Black.

The struggle to define black identity is not the story of one label giving way to a new and universally approved categorical identity. Imagine the appearance of each new term as the splintering or synthesis of what has already gone before. There are many denominations in this church of blackness.

The photo that surfaces at Pardlo holiday dinners shows my great-grandfather "Little Bits." An accident at the Navy Yard left him blind in one eye, like a mystic poet. He could pass for Japanese in the picture, as he sits in a high-backed, clear vinyl-covered chair. Over Little Bits's left shoulder is his son, my grandfather, middle-aged in horn-rimmed glasses, probably not much older, in fact, than I am now. Over Little Bits's right shoulder is his grandson, my father, sporting a solid afro and looking athletic in nut-hugging jeans. In Little Bits's lap is an infant. That, of course, would be me. Four generations of American Otherness: one colored; one Negro; one black; and me, who grudgingly accepts the term "African American." As Carole Boyce Davies notes in her introduction to *Black Women, Writing and Identity,* "African" in "African American" is a term that "attempt[s] to create a monolithic construction out of a diverse continent of peoples, cultures, nations and experiences." For the Romans, Davies suggests, " 'Africa *proconsularis*' was an administrative, territorial category . . . The origin of the term 'Africa' for colonialist, administrative reasons and its subsequent application to an entire continent . . . has implications for how African peoples (particularly in the diaspora) begin to activate monolithic categories of heritage and identity, as, for example, 'Afrocentricity.' " She does not speculate what those implications are, but I surmise she means derivative terms like "Pan-African," terms that unwittingly carry intimations of Eurocentricity. How sadly ironic that our current self-designation, African American, should be derived essentially from a bureaucratic expedient under the earliest of European empires.

We'd like to think we're getting *better* at understanding ourselves, as if each appellation constitutes some stage in development through which we've earned the privilege, like a martial arts belt or an honor badge, to work toward a new name. From Alain Locke's *The New Negro* (1925) to Sherley Anne Williams's "Neo-Black" (1972)* to Trey Ellis's *The New Black Aesthetic* (1989), we've been busily reinventing our-

---

* Despite Williams's reasonable assertion that "neo-black" signals "continuity" with, and a "reinterpretation" of, the black literary tradition, she nonetheless uses the term to flag "the waning of that trend in Black literature in which writers addressed themselves to white audiences." In other words, she uses it to disavow what she perceives to have been a particularly distasteful practice of earlier black writers.

selves, again and again, it seems, in literature and politics, in opposition to our parents. Or trying to.

———

Well into the 1990s, both my father and I would extol the First Black Person to do anything. We found the idea of "firsts" inspiring because we believed there was a chance that we could be the FBP to do something. This also means, of course, that we believed so much in a coherent blackness that we thought being the FBP could bespeak the drive and aspirations of forty million people whose primary organizing principle is the agreement that they would have fared no better, had they been in his shoes, than Homer Plessy on that fateful streetcar.

At heart, my father and I wanted to be like the ancient Roman senators for whom speech and public action were the highest virtue. We were a couple of prospectors staking claims across the untamed expanses of history. This "first fever" that we shared propelled me into idiosyncratic hobbies, pursuits where I was assured some freedom from competition with other African Americans. Instead of football or basketball, I was captain of my high school tennis team. I abandoned writing rap lyrics to study blues and rock guitar, sublimating first-ness into a broader and more nuanced "uniqueness." Opportunity was always double-edged, however, for never far off was the accusation of overreaching: "So what, you think you're going to be the first black Ping-Pong champion?" *Yes,* was always my answer, though usually unspoken, held close like a shiv.

Google "Gregory Pardlo," and you'd think there was only one of us on the planet. This is partly by design, for with what might be construed as a sort of patricidal malice I omitted the "Jr." from my public persona. This follows a succession of other elisions in the family. Had my father's mother, Ollie, not felt betrayed by her father-in-law, Samuel Pardlo, Sr. (Little Bits), for entrusting the house he built in Willow Grove, Pennsylvania, to her sisters-in-law, rather than to her husband, Sam Jr., she might have agreed to name her son Samuel Pardlo III. Inertia would have likely had it, then, that I, too, would be a Samuel Pardlo—the Fourth, I guess. How different would my life have been? Maybe not at all. But I'd have had a far more difficult time "disappearing" three generations of men with whom I shared a name than simply the one. I'd have had to accept that they were a part of me, and for my sanity construct a biographical narrative that proved me the better for it. This is how people get trapped carrying their forebears in a sort of ectoplasmic pregnancy. Ancestor worship is the survival strategy of the dead.

There is, though, at least, one Google return for my name that does not refer to me. It is a letter to the editors at *The New York Review of Books* from an organization calling itself the "American Workers & Artists for Solidarity," of Princeton, New Jersey. The letter, an announcement for a "Solidarity Meeting" on Saturday, February 6, 1982, begins, "Your readers may be interested to know"—euphemistic for *we can't afford to pay for advertising*—and goes on to say:

We invite people to explore how the democratic ideas of the Solidarity movement have relevance to the situation of workers and trade unionists in the United States. Speakers for the event are dissident trade unionists, sympathetic intellectuals and artists, and Solidarity activists. [These include]: Joseph Brodsky, Pete Camarata (Teamsters for a Democratic Union), Miroslav Chojecki of Solidarity, Toy Dixon (Harlan County UMWA), E. L. Doctorow, Alexander Ehrlich, Carlos Fuentes, Allen Ginsberg, Dick Gregory, Nat Hentoff, Greg Pardlo (PATCO), Ed Sadlowski (United Steelworkers), Pete Seeger, Daniel Singer, Dave Skocik (PATCO), Susan Sontag, Studs Terkel, Andrzej Tymowski, Gore Vidal, Kurt Vonnegut, Ben Zemsky (Postal Workers). PEN American Center is a supporting organization.

For a long time, I ignored this search item because "PATCO" appeared after our name. I might have been interested sooner if I'd known this was the event that my father used to brag about so singularly. "I once shared the dais with Gore Vidal," he would say, as if that detail alone made him exceptional. I'm sure he appreciated that the dais was chockablock with intellectual heavyweights, but he admired none more than Vidal, whose manner and wit my father took as a model.

———

One of the more destructive ideas to be planted in the souls of black folk is that of the Talented Tenth. At the heart of this DuBoisian notion is the idea that the preeminent members of the African American population should be responsible for shattering stereotypes; for role-modeling behavior to foster social and economic stability and decrease degeneracy among the rabble; and for advancing the estimation of the race in the eyes of our global and historical contemporaries. Not only does such implicit responsibility approve a divisive elitism already expressed through color consciousness, but it also places an overwhelming burden on anyone either worthy or simply conceited enough to believe her or himself above average. In theory, the Talented Tenth is a self-selecting elite club, which, as a preteen, I was inclined to join, if only because it allowed me to reconcile my father's arrogance with a socially approved form of exceptionalism. But I could only achieve this self-election to the Talented Tenth by abstracting myself from the black masses, by deciding I was superior to 90 percent of the people in the very community responsible for shaping my social identity. Even as I was engaged in the contradictory acts of claiming affinity and pulling rank, then, I had to avoid the logic that my superiority was founded upon others' inferiority.

At the same time, every affirmation I received as a child was taxed by the kingdom of blackness. Each time I acted out I was reminded that the daily comforts I enjoyed—the liberty I thought mine by birth—had cost the lives and dignity of untold millions. Was it any wonder I had concluded there must be a special circle of hell reserved for black children who selfishly expressed their individuality without complying with the ethnographic imperative to "represent"—that great catalyst of racial advancement? At some point I took an oath not to go on strike against my blackness, having concluded it was immoral to strike against that background. And so, every joint I smoked, every beer I downed, every white girl in a halter top I would cause to giggle and blush, I would self-consciously rue, as if this latest trespass were a loogie hawked on the graves of ancestors who'd asked only that my health, happiness, and prosperity prove their countless sacrifices worthwhile. Double bind upon double bind, each effort to liberate myself from the obligations of blackness would redound with anxiety, forcing me to seek comfort deeper yet in the unstable certainties of race. The result was an enshrined self-loathing.

———

In *The Wretched of the Earth,* Fanon writes that the colonized person desires to sleep with the master's wife, preferably in the master's own bed. Detractors point to this as evidence that progressive racial agendas inevitably conceal a spirit of rapine and vice. Granted, Fanon, like the mad genius he was, let some far-out shit get into his work, but I'm certain we are not meant to take him quite literally here. Surely, "the master's wife" is more archetypal than she is real. Soon as we put a real person in her place, the spell is broken.

Fanon relays, too, in *Black Skin, White Masks,* an anecdote containing more folk wisdom than fact: "a coal-black Negro, in a Paris bed with a 'maddening' blonde, shouted at the moment of orgasm, 'Hurrah for Schoelcher!'" It was Victor Schoelcher, Fanon reminds us, who persuaded the French Third Republic to abolish slavery. Fanon reads this obviously unsubstantiated if popular tale as evidence that the body politic of oppressed people might equate the experience of emancipation with *jouissance.*

———

After the jury verdict in the Trayvon Martin case, drummer for the Roots and late-night television bandleader Ahmir "Questlove" Thompson posted on Facebook a response in which he claimed the verdict confirmed for him and for all black men in America that "Trayvon Martin and [He] Ain't Shit." Thompson's post was picked up and adapted for publication in *New*

York magazine. The resulting essay includes an anecdote in which Questlove finds himself coming home one night and sharing an up-elevator in his luxury Harlem high-rise building with an attractive white woman. There are hints of frustrated desire and romantic ambition. The woman, Questlove notes parenthetically, was "bangin,'" and he was like, "*bow chicka wowow.*"

"There are, like, five to eight guards on duty 24/7," in this building, Questlove reports, with "Oscar-winners and kids of royalty and sports guys and mafia goombahs" as neighbors. Nonetheless, at six-two and three hundred pounds, and sporting what he describes as an "uncivilized Afro" (in a *Rolling Stone* interview he describes himself as a "primitive exotic"), he says people still tend to fear him. So it should surprise no one that when offering to play elevator operator, and even calling her "ma'am" as he asks this ostensible neighbor what floor she needs, she does not respond. According to Quest, the woman stands there shrinkingly, as he uses his security card to select his own floor. Although he claims to be more interested in playing Candy Crush on his phone, he notices the rebuke enough to be offended. He is hurt. And this, too, is understandable.

The woman cringes in fear, if for no other reason than that she has spent a lifetime negotiating a culture of violence against women. Peeking nervously at the back of an uncivilized 'fro was for her, no doubt, like glimpsing mute oblivion. Which of them holds power in this moment? That is, which of them is responsible for the emotional labor of managing her fear? Some would say history has proven repeatedly that a black man alone in an elevator with a white woman can't contribute to the official record of what does or does not happen between them, nor to the interpretation of that account. Quest writes the Facebook post partly to subvert this disadvantage. He doesn't want to sleep with her any more than he wants to mug her. I wonder if the last thing he wants is for her to look him in the eye and force the both of them to contend with the figments they have made of one another. What frustrates him—what would frustrate me—is surely not her lack of acknowledgment so much as her resistance to the Princess/Prize type he wishes to project onto her—her refusal to perform even her unattainability as she resists his chivalrous overture, and his desire to bear her symbolically skyward to the tower's penthouse.

I try to limit my compulsive—some might say reckless—eyeballing of strangers in crowds. I admit I find the torrent of eye contact I can make while walking along a midtown Manhattan sidewalk crowded with tourists from around the world somewhat orgiastic—the ecstasy and horror of seeing and being seen by hundreds, each encounter singular and fleeting like a snowflake melting on my nose. I try to rationalize it. Could looking people in the eye have some iconoclastic effect in the sense that one look, like the beam from a lighthouse, might pierce the fog of preconception, and show people a clearer way to relate to others? Why I would need to do this, and what benefit it would serve mankind, I don't know, honestly. Even when it elicits a smile or a nod hello, there's no way to tell if the eye contact has any salutary effects without dissolving the daydream of speculation by stopping to ask, "Excuse me, do you think the eye contact I just made with you will cause you to relate more equitably with your fellow human?" And so I keep searching, not entirely knowing what it is I'm looking for.

Colored People's Time

Don't expect a straight line. My canvas is time, and I can't—don't want to—approach the thing using its own logic, through the pretense of a single discrete, authoritative position. I need to come at it from different angles—a kind of gestalt approach—which means I'll be flinging ideas at it from around the room.

The notion that time should be measured from a single location seems to me patriarchal and oppressive. Actually, the word I'm trying to avoid, because it sounds even more jargony than "patriarchal," is "hegemonic." I feel fettered by Western time, and want some payback for its having underwritten a culture that has saddled me with so much shame. I want to make a case for following my own circadian rhythms, to be a free spirit, but in a way that does not expose me to charges of irresponsibility and poor self-government. I mean to free myself from the fear of those charges.

If, in general, I take pains to be punctual and to situate myself within esteemed traditions, this is born from a fear of being associated with the stereotypes of laziness and bad credit that continue to dog black folks at all levels of personal achievement. Bad credit results from moral failings, I used to think, and would, if I let myself be so stigmatized, prove my inability to master "primitive" impulses I might not be able to discern but certainly knew to fear. I used to want to belong—to America—in a way that would sacrifice every today for an eagerly anticipated tomorrow. Now I'd just like to imagine an America that will allow me to enjoy life in the moment.

During my adolescence, my parents, my brother, and I suddenly found ourselves financially insecure. We lived in what was, at the time, a predominantly white middle-class community where each of our neighbors' homes seemed a yodel away from Swiss predictability. I wanted to emulate my friends' and neighbors' enviably secure and stable families. And during those formative, pubertal years I despised my parents for dragging me down with their misfortunes, their low birth. I wish I could say I'm over it. Most Saturday mornings I sweep the sidewalk in front of my Brooklyn brownstone, remembering the phalanxes of lawnmowers that would resound in unison those venerable Saturdays as I was growing up as surely as the Wagnerian choruses of cicadas ratcheting up their songs of call and response, come evenings, across the neighborhood thick with shrubs and darting rabbits.

My wife, Ginger, and I bought our brownstone in the Bedford-Stuyvesant neighborhood in 2005. The day we closed, our real estate agent took us to dinner at a Korean restaurant in Queens. She said she'd neglected to get us the traditional Korean housewarming gifts of toilet paper and laundry soap, but urged us to ask the spirits of the house for their blessing before we settled in. It's more than a century old, the house, and our new neighbors were not shy about lading us with the lore of its past owners like gift baskets of fruit and wine: people have died in our home.

Many remember Miss Bailey, for example, whose parents bought the house, according to popular guesses, sometime in the 1930s, though voting records show a Bailey at our address as early as 1919. She was felled by a heart attack while tending the hyacinths, lilacs, hydrangeas, and azaleas that are native to these stoops and little front gardens. Homes lined like leather-bound spines in the stacks. Some stained-glass transoms above parlor windows still take cover under tin-snipped lids. Stoops on the north side, punctuated by ornamental balustrades, spill directly on the sidewalk. On our side, the sidewalks are lined with decorative iron railings.

Our neighbor's late father owned our house, and kept it as an income property before the crack-addled eighties. When he died, the house fell into disrepair, trusted to squatters who promised not to set it afire. There are no records for however many walking dead in those years claimed space beneath the roof that is now ours. Kim, the medical doctor who rescued the house, developed complications from a bug bite and succumbed after returning home from one of her many safaris. Then the house sat vacant for a year or so until we bought it in an estate sale. These stories of "before we lived here" made me think about what would be told "after we're gone."

Until we moved to Bed-Stuy, the idea of home for me existed in a timeless present. People didn't die in houses in Willingboro, New Jersey, the suburb of Philadelphia where I grew up. At least not in the 1970s. They moved to Cherry Hill. In Willingboro, there was a sense that within one or two generations the prefab houses themselves would be consumed, all the way down to their concrete slab foundations. Brooklyn brownstones, on the other hand, they're institutions. Ginger and I didn't just move into a building and take on a mortgage the way my parents once had; we became caretakers of an edifice belonging to a different order entirely, and my relationship to space transformed accordingly.

With the landscape no longer disposable, I grew sensitive to space-defining features of the neighborhood: my Luxor Obelisk, my Washington Monument, my *Tour Eiffel.* As if it were a quirk of OCD, I began to index landmarks that would mediate my identification with Brownstone Brooklyn. And in the absence of structures that enjoy the leisure of existing mostly to organize space (fountains or gazebos), I turned to landmarks preoccupied with their own utility: churches, armories. But shrines to God left me about as cold as those faux fortresses crenellated like broken zippers. I became obsessed with the public clock.

In Philadelphia, where my deepest dreamscape sprouts a thicket of clock-topped towers, stands Independence Hall, home of the Liberty Bell, which was displaced by clock faces in the steeple. Another clock tower features a full-scale statue of William Penn and is nicknamed "Big Penn."

The public clock stands as a surrogate for family clocks, the heirloom type that symbolizes a consistent and orderly familial rhythm, the kind of rhythm that didn't exist in my childhood home. The families I envied as I was growing up ate dinner together at the same time every night. They had bedtime routines. Their ancestors lived among them in their sense of tradition, their ritual ordering of time. They owned grandfather clocks. Perhaps my claim to public clocks allowed me to sublimate my envy of those families and channel it into civic awareness, the better to claim all of Brooklyn as my family.

Before there was a stately clock in my house, I took comfort in the fact that Brooklyn was chock-full of them.

———

When my dad didn't want the grandfather clock spending another winter in the storage unit he'd rented after my parents' divorce, I offered to give it a home. It was an automatic response, like offering my seat on the subway to a pregnant woman, but I suppose I'd also felt obligated because, in one of his rare moments of financial liquidity, my dad had chipped in five grand—which we repaid—for the down payment on our house. I rented a moving van for the job of transporting the grandfather clock from the self-storage facility in Willow Grove. When the inquisitive clerk at the rental counter asked what I would be moving, my first reaction was to wonder if he interrogated all customers like this. What did he think I would be moving, stolen television sets? My reaction was a symptom of the PTSD I've developed from a lifetime of abiding strangers' unprocessed racial aggressions. After recentering myself, I could almost see, while I responded, the episode of *Antiques Roadshow* he was scripting in his mind: A nebbishy black guy discovers, in the grandfather clock he's inherited, a hand-drawn map tracing routes between homes and churches across Ohio. Inscribed on it somewhere is "For H.T." Or perhaps the clock's bespectacled appraiser traces its provenance to some early-twentieth-century black banker from Tulsa, a pioneer of black achievement.

Of course, these were my own fantasies, which I projected onto this name-tagged clerk in a car rental office. They said more about my self-image—what I suppose occupies the minds of others as they contemplate me. It's curious that I imagined my clerk segregating my world, as if for him any antique in the hands of an African American would inevitably reveal a history of interest primarily to African Americans. Why didn't I imagine the clerk imagining that the clock had been handed down from some guilt-ridden white ancestor?

Curious, too, that both of my imaginary *Antiques Roadshow* episodes sidestepped more common representations of the black experience. I *didn't* make reference to violence or poverty in the hood. The histories I alluded to—the Underground Railroad and Black Wall Street—endorsed narratives central and dear to the black bourgeoisie. I was distancing myself from the black urban poor as if those two class identities were my only options.

In any event, I could find no evidence of the grandfather clock in my childhood memories. I could trace my paternal line back four generations in the greater Philadelphia area (through my mother I could go back seven), but material possessions are like blossoms on my family tree, flowering with each branching only to vanish within the season.

My father had doubled-dipped the mortgage on the Willow Grove house, the house built by my great-grandfather Little Bits, who made his living at the Philadelphia Naval Yard, where he worked as a rigger on the USS *Wisconsin* during the Second World War. The third steward of the property, my dad, almost immediately siphoned off what available equity there was to be had. Between the market crash of 2008 and the divorce, it was easier for him simply to empty the house, put its contents in storage, and leave the rest to be sorted out by the banks and the raccoons.

My curiosity about the clock's bequest turned to panic as I considered the very real possibility (the probability—this is my father I'm talking about) that the clock might not even work. I shuddered at the potential waste of time and money involved in schlepping a useless monolith certain to unbalance the already haphazard feng shui of my living room. If, on top of that, the clock didn't work, well, it would reproach me whenever I looked at it. I'd hear it calling me lazy. Shiftless.

There is no greater measure of a man than his ability to keep a promise. I'm not sure how much I believe this. It may only be a standard I hold my father to (you live by the gender specificity, you die by it), but I'll go ahead and put it out there for now. And one root, elemental index of that man's human credit rating is the quality of his stewardship of the objects he's inherited from previous generations, that stewardship being a promise of continuity to both the ancient and the unborn, a covenant of sorts. The glue of patriarchal civilization.

There was no reason to assume the clock belonged to my great-grandfather. The man was not big on possessing anything other than real estate. Little Bits arrived in Philadelphia with a trunk containing no memorabilia of his prior life in South Carolina, save for the photograph of a white man who looked an awful lot like him. Little Bits allegedly refused to share any details of his origins or life before he adopted Philadelphia as his home and married a dark-skinned woman, doubtless a proxy for the woman in the photo that should have accompanied his white father's—the photo that was never taken. With what knowledge of home-building he raised the family house in Willow Grove, I have no idea. Little Bits didn't want me to see or to have his history.

You would think there was no Pardlo before him. Establishing himself as the head of the line, Little Bits subjected his history to *damnatio memoriae,* that ancient Roman practice of wiping rivals and foes off the record of human consciousness by seizing their lands and destroying historical records of their existence—statues, documents, debts. This was a common practice among the early-twentieth-century black refugees from the American South, a practice that made of the South—for me—a place as mythical as El Dorado or Atlantis.

———

No one I know uses that word, "shiftless," yet it bugs me just the same. The word is rooted in my fantasy of the American South. The cradle of American slavery and the civil rights movement, Dixie has always ruled over me, a distant empire brought no closer for its persistent presence in the mind. The antidote to shiftlessness is encapsulated in a line of W. E. B. DuBois's I cling to in defiance: "I shirk not. I long for work. I pant for a life of striving."[*] In the medley of a pep talk I give myself before daunting tasks, the words harmonize with Whitman's, "I am the man, I suffered, I was there." It's a theme song of inspirational quotes I play myself, a habit I picked up from my father.

My father's example is the storm on the horizon I don't want to lose sight of and can't let myself get close to. A lifetime of calibrating these perils of proximity gives me credentials in a kind of metaphysical math, a telemetry of spiritual disaster. Compulsively, at times, I have insinuated myself into the drama of that disaster or failed to distinguish myself from it and so mirrored its black boot as if it were my true inheritance.

---

[*] *The Souls of Black Folk* (1903).

Ginger and I are friends with a rabbi whose kids are close in age to our kids. At a play date once I asked her why we inflict the stories of suffering and human cruelty we inherit on our children. In the Stephen Dunn poem "At the Smithville Methodist Church," two parents are conflicted after the first day of arts and crafts week at the church they've sent their daughter to. The girl comes home with a "Jesus Saves" button. They're not religious, but the kid likes the camp. Although they're embarrassed by all the singing and the "jump[ing] up and down / for Jesus" their kid is doing, the dad concludes, as my dad would paraphrase it, *resistance is futile*. The Bible is a more exciting story than evolution. "You can't say to your child," Dunn writes, " 'Evolution loves you.' The story stinks / of extinction and nothing // exciting happens for centuries."

This is how assimilation happens. We understand how much of a difference a strong narrative can make in someone's life, but we aren't willing to write those narratives ourselves. We don't often have the fortitude to believe in a narrative that isn't validated by institutions, park statues, or long-standing traditions and rituals. It's difficult to hold on to a history that provides no immediate material advantage beyond the feel-good embrace of home. We shrug our shoulders and accept what everyone else is accepting. Selling out is the convenient thing to do.

If I'd rather not raise my kids on a story, like Black History, that has been handed down in a way that foregrounds sadness and frustration, what can I give them in its place? The rabbi told me that the story of the Jews, too, is a story of survival and endurance. But the story of the black American, because it has an identifiable originating event—the Big Bang of the Middle Passage—is difficult to spin as inspiring or promising unless we give the story a biblical version of evil. We make black people Good and slave owners Bad. In this reduction, the Bad Man gets polished to an obdurate, inhuman sheen while the suffering endured by the meek is given a purpose: the meek must nobly endure, anticipating their inheritance, while the Bad Man stands outside the possibility of redemption. Unlike institutional racism, which is both measurable and real, the Bad Man is a ghost who answers to no legislation or public policy, and obscures the messy truth that America is an ideological collaboration, a work in progress undertaken simultaneously from countless points of view. I want my kids to do more than endure, as difficult as I know it is to do that alone.

"You need a Torah," the rabbi suggested, which is a great idea, except that black history is the director's cut of American history. We need to eliminate the idea that we can attend to one without having to attend to the other. We need something concrete, a unifying symbol—not a flag—that neither requires nor begs interpretation. I later realized I was looking for a grandfather clock to stand for my spite-free dream of ancestry.

———

Before I first traveled to Dixie, the South had been for me little more than a series of stories organized like a shelf in the stacks, beginning with Thomas Jefferson's *Notes on the State of Virginia,* published in 1785, and ending with Jean Toomer's modernist novel, *Cane,* published in 1923. Between these bookends was a textual landscape brought to life by my imagination, a place overrun with kudzu and chifforobes and grandfather clocks.

In 2002, Ginger and I announced our engagement, and began to analyze the nature of marriage. For me it seemed a way to control women's reproductive power and ensure the legitimacy of men's heirs—why I never had children with my first wife, Maya. For Ginger, it was a ritual framework that gave social meaning to affective bonds. *From This Day Forward,* the Cokie Roberts book Ginger was using as her theoretical guide, offered popular insights on building a strong marital foundation. I, however, was reluctant to take advice from Cokie or her husband, Steve, despite how affable they seemed in their cover photo. Ginger quoted from the book at length. Because Ginger's family is Salvadoran and mine African American, she was interested in how Cokie and Steve had negotiated their thirty-year interfaith marriage. Only the defining difference between Ginger and me is nothing as simple as that.

If I have committed to be somewhere at a given time, the one failure that would call my self-worth into question would be to arrive late or—it offends me even to acknowledge the possibility—not at all. Ginger, on the other hand, will be late getting someplace she's already *at.* Yet Ginger is the hardest-working vacationer I've known. No lounging by the pool when Ginger's around. Her daily itineraries are overly ambitious lesson plans. One more church. One more fish market or factory floor. There is no rest until we are thoroughly weary of factoids, unable to hold between thumb and forefinger the thread of consciousness that links us to whatever grand spectacular she promises to lay before us next.

Something in the Cokie Roberts book gave Ginger the idea that if we hoped to raise children who would have a sense of the richness of their multiplex heritage, we needed to make pilgrimages to our ancestral homelands to make personal, first-hand connections with our ancestry. We needed our boots on

the ground. And so we arranged to spend, first, two weeks
traveling through Central America, enjoying the hospitality of
Ginger's relatives when possible, and then, following that, a
civil rights tour of the American South.

We claimed the spirit of the Freedom Riders of 1961, but
stayed in B&Bs approved by AAA. We flew into Atlanta, where
we rented a car. From there we drove east to Charleston, South
Carolina, then south to Savannah, Georgia, before heading
west for Montgomery and north to Birmingham in Alabama,
then east again back to Atlanta. We had hoped to make a stop
in Selma before returning to Atlanta, but were—surprise—
short on time, and there were still more museums in Atlanta
we had put off for the return visit.

One of our more enlightening whistle stops was the Aiken-
Rhett House, a uniquely preserved town house of one of
Charleston's wealthy slave owners, the sixty-first governor,
William Aiken, Jr. The house was organized and operated
like a semi-urban plantation, its product being not cotton or
tobacco, but rather (it seemed to me) the master's leisure, prestige, and consequential ennui. Women of the master's class
engaged in handcrafts of such baroque detail—involving feath-
ers and bone, buttons, silk, and other arcane bric-a-brac—
that they seemed practiced expressly for their depletion of
time. The slaves, on the other hand, occupied every integer
on the production line of domesticity, from shoeshine to chef;
the property's expansive gardens (occupying a space roughly a
quarter the size of Washington Square Park, as I recall), live-
stock, and interdict against production-side waste made it a
model of green living the twenty-first century could envy. Of
course there were luxury objects: the concert harp, the chif-
forobe. Of particular interest, the guide pointed out, was the

estate's grandfather clock. A symbol of prestige, the clock was a symbol of the master's control over time, wresting from nature the rhythm of all quotidian activity—domestic, communal, and artisanal. No mere symbol, though, this master's clock mastered time *in fact*.

———

It had been eight years since Ginger and I had taken our "civil rights tour" of the South when, in 2010, my father decided to liquidate the storage unit, and I stood to "inherit," as my father saw it, the grandfather clock. The sense of fidelity owed to our respective ethnicities had long since faded, and our zeal for establishing traditions unique to our new, shared family given way to the exigencies of daily life with two small children. We could barely keep Friday's regular pizza night. An heirloom grandfather clock was the last thing we needed. Without thinking about it, I had begun a process of passively forgetting my past, like so many cheap umbrellas, to make way for the present. I had begun to convince myself my identity was being shaped by environment alone. *Ich bin ein Brooklyner.* And yet here was that clock now, exerting its tractor beam of a claim on me, dragging me back into its past before even arriving in our home.

———

An inoperative public clock says a great deal not only about the community it is supposed to serve. If we put any stock in the "broken windows theory" of criminology—which holds that if something as seemingly minor as a broken window is left unrepaired for a long enough time, it can set norms of disorder, and signal permissiveness for all manner of civil trespass—then we can only guess at how broad the repercussions on a community of something as centrally visible as a broken public clock.

The Williamsburgh Savings Bank clock, with its four twenty-seven-foot faces once the world's largest (Big Ben's faces being a paltry twenty-three feet in diameter), rises 512 feet on what had been, until the completion of an ambitious residential skyscraper downtown in 2009, the tallest structure in Brooklyn. Completed in 1929, the office tower, with its gilt dome soaring over the basilica of the bank lobby that juts out on either side to form the base, evoking ecclesiastical as well as priapic sturdiness, is intended to associate banking with spiritual practice as much as the latent erotics of free-market competition. Intended, according to the building's architects, as "a cathedral dedicated to the furtherance of thrift and prosperity," it is meant to blur distinctions between the sacred and profane.

In 2005, the year Ginger and I bought our brownstone and had our first child, the Williamsburgh Savings Bank, at the edge of the Fort Greene neighborhood of Brooklyn, was purchased by a group of investors led by Magic Johnson, a move that betokened the even further Manhattanization of the borough as the investors intended to convert thirty-four floors of office space into high-end condos.

By my calculation Fort Greene officially became a "black neighborhood" sometime around 1966. Though I have it on good authority that Fort Greene was predominantly black well before '66, I place the neighborhood's ethnic birth date here for literary reasons. This is the year Fort Greene's famous resident the poet Marianne Moore decamped for less diverse environs across the East River, and it aligns cleanly with 2006 (fudging, for convenience's sake, the date of the bank building's Magic rebirth). In the forty-year period between Moore's departure and Magic's arrival, the "Big Willy" clock, as it is popularly known, was at best an unreliable timepiece. But in 2006, by which point, it is safe to say unequivocally, speculators had conquered Fort Greene, Big Willy was restored as a fully illumined beacon of communal synchrony. One of the clock's custodians at the time of the repair happily reported, "If the clock is off, people will come in and tell us, 'Your clock was off and I was late for work.'" The return of capital investment may have been foreseeable, and some people look to the appearance of coffee shops and dog runs as reliable indicators, but the truest sign of an entrenched gentrification is the return of common time.

There are smaller-scale clocks, too, that interest me. The former Bond Bread factory on Flatbush and Ocean, for example, which long housed a Phat Albert's wholesale outlet. Or the Dime Savings Bank digital clock that, with its casement rusted like the hull of an abandoned tanker ship, might still greet motorists coming off of the Manhattan Bridge onto the Flatbush Avenue Extension in Brooklyn, if not for the new highrise obscuring it. Before the construction boom, Washington Mutual acquired the building and covered with huge strips of correction tape the word "Dime" above the neon numbers of the clock. Then JPMorgan Chase took over Washington Mutual and affixed to the sign's crusty girders the Chase logo, ignoring the number display altogether.

I started judging banks—as harshly as I judge people who flip houses in vulnerable neighborhoods—for the quality of their stewardship of the timepieces that come along with the properties they acquire. When a bank fails to maintain the clock on one of its buildings, I know its presence in the community is temporary. The bank's responsibility is to faraway shareholders, rather than to time-bound local account holders.

We knew, in 2005, there was a land rush in Brooklyn, and that owning a home was possible if one was willing to buy in a distressed neighborhood. Our friends Jason and Michael were on the market, too. They led us further into the hood—with its cracked sidewalks and open-air drug markets—than we would have braved on our own. You couldn't have mistaken Ginger and me for savvy homebuyers, no matter how tactical our investment may seem in retrospect. We didn't choose to buy in Bedford-Stuyvesant; Bed-Stuy's indifferent availability acted like an economic baleen capturing even the krill of our demographic heft and hue.

We didn't know that banks were handing mortgages out with the lollipops. What was otherwise a global financial crisis was for us a lucky break. It was like that Eddie Murphy sketch "White Like Me," where Murphy spends a day undercover as a white man. Our loan officer didn't toss our application and hand us wads of cash instead, the way the loan officer in the sketch does, but the process for us was no less absurd. "Pay us back when you want," Murphy's loan officer says. "Or don't!" We were, Ginger and I, afforded the kind of privilege I'd always dreamed of getting, the benefit of the doubt. I thought I'd finally made it. I didn't want to be white; I wanted all the shit I thought comes with it. We should have known something was wrong when our mortgage broker asked what we thought our salary would be in a few years. Ginger had gotten pregnant between jobs and decided that was as good a maternity leave as she was likely to get. She put off the job search until after the baby was born. Still, it didn't matter that I was the only one of us employed in 2005. Pay stubs from her former employer were good as T-bills for the mortgage guy. Adding to my father's gift, my mother-in-law ponied up another five grand. Ginger and I scraped what we could out of our retirement accounts, and miraculously all sufficed for a down payment. We didn't plan to stay in Bed-Stuy for the long term, but we did, and soon were looking down our noses at all the transient renters and flippers exploiting our beloved community.

II

Each morning I reached Adinkra* College in Brooklyn, where I taught for six years, by walking down the hill from the subway station toward the intersection referred to as "campus." I was greeted by the main building, a split-level, glazed brick low-rise with a trapezoidal tower that had been raised as a symbolic message to Crown Heights's shrinking population of West Indians and African Americans. Stuck on 11:10, the miming hands of the clock tower presented an effigy of time, a travesty of the bonds communal rhythms make possible, a refusal to capitulate to the dominant cultural perception of duration. The Adinkra clock tower announced what I think is ultimately a resistance to assimilate on even the most fundamental terms.

One of the mainstays on my syllabus at the time was Charles Johnson's novel *Middle Passage*. Johnson's free black protagonist, Rutherford Calhoun, muses on the fate of an African tribal god that has been captured and stowed in the cargo hold of the slave ship Calhoun has unknowingly (and comically) smuggled himself onto as a crew member in order to escape

---

* I have changed the name of the college.

marriage to a woman intent on domesticating him. Also held captive on the ship are members of the tribe that worships this god; these people, the fictional Allmuseri, are depicted as such an ancient people that they have effectively passed *through* the need for accumulated knowledge, "as if longevity . . . had made them . . . a clan distilled from the essence of everything that came earlier." In other words, they have whetted their core values, beliefs, and traditions against all imaginable systems of thought and social organization over so many generations that they appear to Calhoun as a kind of "Ur-tribe of humanity." According to Calhoun, the Allmuseri "were so incapable of abstraction no two instances of 'hot' or 'cold' were the same for them, this hot porridge today being so specific, unique, and bound to the present that it had only a nominal resemblance to the hot porridge of yesterday." They lived *literally*. That is, in the moment.

The Allmuseri god, a living object I imagine to be something like the anthropomorphic grandfather clock in Alice's Wonderland, is given paradoxical powers, being physically present and everywhere at once. These powers allow it to shape-shift and appear differently according to the temperament of each person encountering it, such that it cannot be objectively "known," and yet is material enough to be controlled and held captive. It is rather like a book, in fact, in that it exists at once here and everywhere, but also in the way that we can censor or burn the book only after we have read it and determined it to be dangerous. The book can't be unread and the god can't be undisclosed. Were such a god, simultaneously a barrier and a conduit, unleashed on the culturally adolescent West, "History as we knew it," Calhoun suggests, "would *end,* for there would be no barriers between the secular and sacred."

Differences in cultural perceptions of time come down, in the end, to how and to what extent we distinguish between sacred and secular. Westerners, lacking the eidos—which, more than just the cultural character of a group, has an active quality, and is what someone is referring to when they say *that's how we roll*—Westerners are not conditioned to conceive of the sacred and the secular as a unified, fluid mode of awareness. We create grand taxonomies of difference and then expend great effort convincing ourselves that these abstractions are real. This is obvious in our inventions of race and other forms of identity, but also in our structuring of time.

In a gross generalization of a continent brimming with cultural differences, Richard Wright, in *Black Power,* writes of African time: "It was a circular kind of time; the past had to be made like the present." While the Nigerian Nobel laureate Wole Soyinka calls it "a cyclic reality . . . which denies periodicity to the existences of the dead, the living and the unborn." So deeply rooted is the cyclic conception of time in the cultural practices of Yoruban society that we may safely view it as an epistemological fact of that culture. Indeed, to the extent that circular time in so-called pagan cultures preceded and coexists with "In the beginning" linearity, Christianity's Judaic tradition seems to be the minority view.

It is possible newly arrived American slaves in the late eighteenth and nineteenth centuries[*] had to reconcile, as a condition of their limited though compulsory assimilation, both extremes of time awareness. Speculatively, kidnapped Africans could have brought with them, on one hand, an eidos that viewed time as circular and ritualistic. On the other hand, to

---

[*] Earlier arrivals from Africa would have encountered a society that still thought of itself as colonial and therefore indebted to alien measures of time.

be naturalized as slaves, so to speak—that is, to be remade as proto–American Negroes—they would have had to reconfigure that eidos in order to accept the contrary view of time enforced by plantation rule, which is time-as-linear-duration, working from can't-see-in-the-morning until can't-see-at-night, as the saying goes, with random interruptions, marking time irregularly with the lash, their teleological sights trained on the singularly distant prospect of deliverance in the next world.

What trauma might such a process of transformation have wreaked on early African Americans? And how might remnants of that pre–Middle Passage African mind have survived, sewn into the hems of garments, baked into pies, mixed into the narrative mortar of American culture?

Atavistic perceptions of time survive in black America. Our misunderstanding of these perceptions reinforces negative assumptions of what it means to *be* black in America. What could arguably have been a benign disregard for abstraction in the pre-slavery African mind, for example, would have been perceived by plantation overseers in America as no more than stubborn indolence. Put in yet another way, the propensity to disregard public time that evolved in response to the trauma of slavery, and which in the African American community is facetiously referred to as *CP time*, or "colored people's time," need not be seen simply as a confirmation of the racist presumption that black folks are by nature lazy or recalcitrant. Plumbing this temporal disposition may allow me to indulge in my own creative leisure without racial guilt or self-loathing.

Let's say I had had an answer for that curious clerk at the car rental place. Why should it matter how long the clock had been in my family? As it turned out, it was my grandfather Sam Jr. and not my great-grandfather Little Bits who'd bought the thing. Sam Jr. got it at Pier 1 Imports in the 1990s. There was a store closing and a subsequent blowout sale replete with plastic banners flapping across a parking lot. Sam Jr., who fancied himself a shrewd consumer, could not resist a sale. When I got the clock home, I found it still had the instruction manual in plastic at the bottom of its encasement, along with the coiled electrical cord.

In addition to keeping time now, as it hums through the evenings at the top of the steps in the Bed-Stuy brownstone that is our family home, it is good for lighting the hallway, its big broad Roman numerals lit up like slivers of the moon, a beacon in the dark I look up to each night on my way to bed.

Private School

Ginger and I took seats house left along the aisle of the Boyce Auditorium in Intermediate School 383, a "Gifted and Talented" public middle school in Bushwick, Brooklyn. Her equipment—projector and screen, plus an enormous cardboard box full of brochures and bright yellow pencils and clear plastic rulers with simple shapes cut out of their middles, and magnets, all the giveaways bundled in rubber bands—obstructed the aisle. While she waited for the PTA meeting to begin, Ginger counted the bundles, and then counted again.

In addition to benefits fairs and new-hire orientations, for her new job, Ginger would target PTA meetings fertile with parents nerve-wracked over the impending costs of their kids' college education. Ginger conducted informational sessions to promote the state-sponsored and tax-sheltered 529 College Savings plan. Her territory covered New York City, parts of Westchester County, and Long Island. There were hundreds more schools in more affluent areas she could cold call, but she had been trying for months to get into 383.

"My wife is in finance," I often told people as a way to extract some usable social currency. More precisely, she was a "relationship manager," and didn't make much money. No commissions. No bonuses. The state contracted out to the company Ginger worked for, which made her subject to rules governing state employees, so her only real incentive was social change. This, fortunately, was enough. This, and the perks of being able to work from home, to set her own schedule and accommodate the demands of family life.

"My wife is in sales," I might have said, alternatively. She sold her clients something they already had, a version of the American Dream half-forgotten, like a yoga mat in the back of the closet.

"We all know," Ginger began, in a version of the speech she regularly gave to the group she'd been invited to address, "how difficult it is to become financially secure in one generation." When I'd heard her speak in the past, I'd thought she was dry, too corporate. At 383, she scrapped the generic pitch as I'd encouraged her to do. "As a young woman, my mother immigrated to this country from El Salvador. She knew little English. I grew up translating—in the many senses of the word that people like us are used to, not just language, but culture and those unspoken rules and assumptions and values. Your children know this, too. I see myself in them, and in you. Being here today to talk to you about college and how to pay for it allows me to do what I've always done *entre familia*. Thank you.

"My mother came to this country, like so many of you, for a better future. She left her home, she left her family, she left everything she knew for a better tomorrow. She worked in sweatshops here in New York City. She's been a nanny, and an entrepreneur. She had her own *negocio* in a flea market in SoHo in the eighties. In time, she brought most of her family members here, and helped them get established. My story, the story of my family, is like that of so many of us—we are here in the United States, whether we came here, or our parents or our grandparents did; whether our ancestors were brought here, we are all alike working for a better tomorrow, not just for ourselves, but for all our loved ones.

"When I was eighteen years old, my mother and my grand-mother drove me from Bushwick, Brooklyn, to Boston to drop me off at Harvard College. I'll never forget the day. She didn't know what she could do to help, but my mother was deter-mined to do *something*. She *insisted* on buying me a computer. I didn't understand why at the time. I didn't need a com-puter. Now, I won't tell you my age, but I will tell you that computers were very new when I started college. They were expensive. We were poor. I was fine with using the computer in the library or borrowing my friend's computer to write my research papers. But my mother wouldn't reconsider. She had seen me work hard to get to college. She didn't know entirely what kind of career my studies would lead to. She only knew college meant I would have a more comfortable life than she had growing up in El Salvador. She couldn't give me advice or guidance, but she knew what I was doing was important, and she wanted to contribute.

"You are here today because you see that it is possible for your son or daughter to go to college. This opportunity was not as available to previous generations the way it is today. We know it's not available to many in our home countries, but here in the United States, here today, it is. It is possible. And you want to support that. You might want to buy a computer or books or help with tuition or just help with laundry and care packages. I can tell you these things are important. But there are many ways to help. Some ways, in the long run, are more practical than others. Some American families can prepare their kids for college from birth. Some prepare before their kids are even born. Many American families prepare their children for college several generations before they are born! Those families have an advantage in that regard. I'm here to help you get some of that advantage. When it comes time to pay for college, where does the money come from? There is a simple equation: $A + B + C = D$. The final variable, D, is the full cost of college. A is scholarships, B is family contribution, and C is loans. Today we are going to discuss B, your family contribution."

She's an inspiring public speaker, but my wife has lost touch with her roots over the years. I had to insist that she drop the H-bomb in her pitch, because she was so convinced that it was in poor taste to tell people she had gone to Harvard. Ivy League decorum won't translate in working-class communities, I told her. It may be polite to say you went to school in "Cambridge" or "New Haven" instead of just saying the name of the damn school, but any parent willing to bet on a distant and almost unimaginable future for their child wants to see hard evidence of the potential payoff. Her job, after all, was to give her audience proof that class mobility was still possible. They don't want to decipher class codes.

This night, at 383, was no different except that she was speaking—not so coincidentally—to the PTA at the middle school she herself had attended in the late seventies. When she was a student at 383, the population was mixed, black and Latino. The black kids tended to come from Bedford-Stuyvesant, the historically black neighborhood of brownstones nearby where, another non-coincidence, Ginger and I had bought a house some years before. The kids from Bed-Stuy tended to live not in apartments, but in houses with backyards. Some had their own bedrooms, and, often enough, they came from two-parent homes. They seemed more stable and established than families in the tenement buildings of Bushwick, where Ginger lived, and were her earliest models of financial and emotional security. Ginger thought fondly of this school as the first of several turning points in her life. As soon as she'd gotten the job promoting 529s, she imagined herself speaking to parents at 383.

All through elementary school she'd been at the top of her class, but when she got to 383 for middle school, she began to imagine herself enjoying the sort of lifestyle successful sitcom families appeared to enjoy. IS 383 was where she internalized the mandate given to children of the time who were, as Nina Simone said, "young, gifted and black," a mandate that swept her collaterally—considering she is not black—under its maternal apron, instructing her that in order to succeed, she would have to work twice as hard as her white peers, notwithstanding the fact that, outside the context of central Brooklyn, she would be racially indistinguishable from those white peers.

Loretta U. Boyce was the founding principal of IS 383. Boyce was a big woman, as Ginger recalled. Not physically big, but formidable. A pioneering activist, she was fond of reminding children that "to whom much is given, much is expected in return." I, too, knew women like Boyce when I was growing up in suburban South Jersey. It was not uncommon for women like her to leave their native cities to raise high-achieving children in the suburbs. These were the mothers of my own friends and classmates, mothers who often had some nugget of black history to offer me while their kids and I played video games or while we sat at the kitchen counter destroying packages of Chips Ahoy.

Over the preceding weeks, Ginger must have left a pad-ful of "while you were out" messages at the main desk, trying to contact anyone with the authority to schedule her time at any public meeting involving the parents and neighborhood residents. With each call, she mentioned that her name was among the list of valedictorians engraved on a plaque in the main hall. Class of 1982. None of the people who'd answered the phone seemed too impressed by Ginger's achievement. The demographics were changing. The neighborhood was gentrifying, and public schools were losing ground to charters. It was probably these same demographic changes that prompted someone from the school finally to get back to Ginger, and invite her to speak.

On the lookout for Granny, my mother-in-law, who would arrive with our two girls in the inevitable clamor of shopping bags, nerves, and general exhaustion, I surveyed the institutional midcentury modern of Ginger's alma mater, trying to imagine myself as one of Ginger's classmates. How parallel would our lives have run? As a working-class African American, I might have been better suited for this environment than she was. Then again, upon graduating from this G&T public middle school, Ginger was recruited by Dalton, an Upper East Side independent school, and I can't imagine having had the grades or the wherewithal to make such a transition myself.

I try to imagine the strength of character thirteen-year-old Ginger would have needed to survive the contradictions in her life at Dalton after 383. Leaving Bushwick each morning, she had to dismantle herself completely, and reassemble herself

anew prior to entering the Upper East Side prep school building as nannies and chauffeurs bid good day to their charges,
her new peers. The feat is all the more impressive considering
that no matter how much emotional support Ginger's mother
might offer, she never could have entirely imagined the scope
of Ginger's need for that support.

In 1968, having just given birth to her red-haired first child,
my Salvadoran mother-in-law was visited by a life insurance
salesman. If hospitals were more considerate of each patient's
comfort back then, they were also a good deal less fussy about
strange men browsing a ward full of incapacitated new mothers. Her English was rudimentary, but my mother-in-law
understood well enough that the man was asking her to open
a savings account for her child's college tuition. She looked at
the ruddy child in her arms whose hair was bright as a safety
vest, and she could not yet envision a future that might offer
this girl child anything more than a state-mandated education,
not even with the imaginative strength she had summoned to
achieve the dream of a life in this strange city with no friends
or family. "No, thank you," she said, smiling at the man in the
brown suit.

The life Ginger and I had built together was by no means
lavish, which put us at odds with the materialist values of her
mother, who had to look for other ways to make her status as
the immigrant mother of an Ivy League graduate visible. My
mother-in-law would occasionally lie to people. Sometimes
she would tell her coworkers at the day care center where she
worked that her daughter was a lawyer in New York City. Or
she might tell people her daughter *currently* attended Harvard
or Princeton, where Ginger got her master's degree. For many
years, my mother-in-law worked as a nanny, and, though she

never said so, I suspect she was unsettled by her daughter's inability to afford a nanny of her own.

I wanted kids, and Ginger wasn't entirely opposed to the idea. Ginger didn't have an opinion for or against having children. She could manage a sincere "cute!" or "aww," when coworkers showed pictures of their babies, but when forced to, she would handle one of the tentacled incontinent meatballs like it was rigged to explode. I, on the other hand, wasn't afraid to hold a baby to my bosom or bounce one on my knee. As the oldest leaf on my branch of the family tree, I'd seen my cousins being cared for by the women in my family, and I thought this practically qualified me as a doula.

Granny believed children were incapable of deceit. If possible, she would have spent her days surrounded by children and woodland creatures. The innocence she saw in children made them vulnerable to adults, and this vulnerability worried my mother-in-law. When the telenovelas were not available, Granny would channel surf in search of news stories detailing the ravages of *terremotos* and tsunamis. Her television was the altarpiece, in the glass of which she herself was reflected as Our Lady of the Morbid Imagination. She sprayed hair spray at mosquitoes, smeared vapor rub on my children's feet, and refused to use a clothes dryer or dishwasher. She preferred glue to nails. With her arms crossed and her chin in her fist like she was holding an ice cream cone, she would shake her head in grim dismay. After a day of sitting my daughters, whom she had bedecked in ribbons and bows, and dresses pristine and shiny as new linoleum, Granny assumed the chin-fist position when she settled into her seat in Loretta U. Boyce Auditorium to hear Ginger speak.

The girls, smelling faintly of vapor rub, greeted me with

the fervor of besotted hooligans—which elicited disdain-ful looks from the PTA members, followed by some looks of polite indulgence, and one earnestly puckered *"So cute!"* The security guard, however, a thirtysomething Latina, walked over, her keys a-jangle, and told me I couldn't let my kids run around the auditorium. I had to watch them because they might get hurt. "You have two kids," she informed me using her fingers. "You need to take care of them." After which she added, *"Too cute!"*

There's no use getting offended by people who tell me how to raise my kids. Lacking the aversion to conflict that often passes for gentility, the security guard was, in her way, assum-ing familiarity, even offering a kind of blessing, perhaps. In her own way. *Dios las bendiga—so cute!*

———

When it was time to put Sara in school, we decided to send her to the Rudolf Steiner School, a private school on the Upper East Side of Manhattan. There were no acceptable options where we lived, just west of Bushwick, in Bedford-Stuyvesant. Whatever the neighborhood's reputation in the world outside of Ginger's tween geographic purview, the kids from Bed-Stuy were, to her, middle-class New Yorkers. No matter that it had persevered through redlining, gangs, and crack cocaine to emerge as a poster child for gentrification, Ginger's deeply rooted admiration for the historic home of Brooklyn's black bourgeoisie did not mitigate our revulsion at the public schools there. Nearly all of the neighborhood schools then were fail-ing, but our local, or "zone," school was worst of all. Empow-ered and resource-rich families had not yet infiltrated as deeply into the neighborhood as we had, and there wasn't demand enough to warrant either the takeover of an existing school (replacing all the teachers and administrators) or the establishment of a charter.

And so, with the tortured dignity of class-anxious gentrifiers, Ginger and I went on the hunt for an independent school. We attended open houses and, pretending to be as aloof as Secret Service in advance of a presidential visit, reconnoitered. We were eager to identify the level of crass parental hustle to which we would not stoop, although in truth there was none. Still, we scoffed at parents who ardently prepped their toddlers for the Early Childhood Admissions Assessment, the SAT for pre-K.

At the top of our list was Dalton, which I'd never heard of before meeting Ginger. Surprised at how just mentioning the name could cow into submission natives of the private school circuit like the revelation of their god, I was, at least at first, disinclined to trust the hype, but—let's be honest—it's a great school. And if our kid would benefit from being a legacy admission, well, great.

I was surprised at how emotional I got when, at Dalton's open house, the gym teacher described a project he'd coordinated with the social sciences teacher. Students in the "lower school," which I knew as elementary school, were each given pedometers to track the distances they traveled in an average gym class. These distances were then tallied and represented by a thread on a wall map. They extended the thread each day to reflect the collective distance traveled by the class toward a country like, say, Honduras that they were studying in another class. They did this in their gym class. Their *gym* class.

By the end of the gym teacher's presentation, I felt like new evidence had just exonerated me from a twenty-year sentence

I'd already served. My elementary school education gave me no indication that I might encounter the world beyond the Delaware Valley, where my hometown of Willingboro was cradled. I couldn't locate Honduras on a globe until I was in college. At the Dalton open house, I learned my ignorance was not entirely my fault. I knew some teachers were better than other teachers, but I thought that was just a matter of personality. I didn't know that money could buy more than books and desks. Money could buy better means of instruction.

My father threatened to take me out of Twin Hills Elementary School and send me to Valley Forge Military Academy so often I thought that if you didn't go to public school, you went either to boarding school with orphans in France or to some disciplinary academy to learn how to stand in a single-file line. When, after sixth grade, my best friend, Nubie, went to Moorestown Friends instead of Memorial Junior High like the rest of us, I wondered what kind of sadists the Quakers must be to have convinced his parents to send him there. At Twin Hills Elementary, Nubie had been in the reading and math groups for average kids. I'd been in the advanced groups, and took it for granted that I was smarter than him. But in the one year Nubie attended Moorestown Friends he started acting like a smart kid. His vocabulary was suddenly bigger than mine, and he was interested in corny shit like science-fiction books. He got an after-school job at the library. From then on, Friends schools beguiled me.

A colleague of mine, another professor at Adinkra College, had a child Sara's age and was working the independent school scene at the same time Ginger and I were. My colleague was pro-black in a way that I'd always found intimidating. Traditional-African-garb-wearing black. Able-to-say-

As-Salaam-Alaikum-unironically black. She and her husband were determined to get their kid into Brooklyn Friends School. Assessing the situation, Ginger and I decided we didn't have the stamina to keep pace with this family over the long run, as we knew we would compulsively, if unconsciously, strive to do. We decided to avoid Brooklyn Friends, our second choice, if only to maintain a distance from their child, who at the age of three could move us to tears by singing the Ghanaian national anthem in Swahili or whatever. We applied to the Friends School in Manhattan.

Certainly, I didn't want to pass my own envy and self-consciousness on to my child. Intent on finding an environment that was not designed to make her *compete,* at least not too much, not *too* early, I imagined a landscaped campus with sculptures tucked within modest hedge mazes along raked gravel paths, with besmocked children standing before easels at the edge of a well-circulated pond. The problem with utopias, of course, is that they don't exist, but that didn't keep me from dreaming.

In our earlier search for a signature parenting style, both Ginger and I had taken Sara to "Mommy and Me" classes at the Brooklyn Waldorf School and, at least as a three-year-old, Sara responded well to them. We, on the other hand, were freaked out. Each class began with the teachers—young women in flowing skirts and aprons—singing. In fact, they never really *said* anything. Nothing was spoken. The class was like a dour musical performed by Mennonite nuns. We mocked it, but it saved us a lot of grief, that singing. As a joke to break stress, we sang to Sara whenever she had a meltdown; we sang when I burned my thumb on the lasagna pan; when Ginger and I felt an argument coming on, one of us would start to argue our point in song. It worked. Two years later, when Sara was school age, we put Waldorf schools in our top five.

In 1919, the Waldorf-Astoria Cigarette Factory in Stuttgart commissioned Rudolf Steiner to open a school for the children of workers employed there. Steiner's ideas about childhood development were typical of the faux sciences popular at the time. He hoped to explain social abstractions in scientific terms. Steiner promoted what he called a "social threefolding," according to which political, economic, and cultural institutions form the three primary areas of public life. It was the age of phrenology, eugenics, scientific racism, and divisions of labor; Steiner also categorized people and functions and roles, and he mapped that logic, for better or worse, onto students.

A Waldorf education, we learned at the Steiner open house, was meant to address three important faculties within individuals: thinking, feeling, and willing. By marking off these areas of inner life like cuts of beef, Steiner hoped to develop children into more balanced people, as opposed to merely students, shifting the emphasis slightly away from the accumulation of data or utilitarian skill. He believed that a properly educated child would carry the ideological structure of her classroom into adult life, instilling a framework for self-guidance and self-teaching. It was all rather mystifying, but we smiled and nodded before turning back to ogle the marble staircase.

It turned out that Dalton was a bust. The legacy thing didn't work as reliably as I'd hoped. How do you evaluate a five-year-old? You look at things like disposition and emotional security, but you also evaluate the parents. I would have checked my class resentments at the door and not been so smug when we spoke to admissions officers if I had known they were factoring *me* into the equation. Among the wait-lists and acceptances that we did cull from our search, the Waldorf school felt most like home. It was far from a no-brainer. On a yellow legal pad, Ginger and I had drafted lists of what we wanted in a school—the deal-breakers and the things we could compromise on, and we drafted our familial mission statement: *Social equality through education. Freedom to create and innovate safe from financial insecurity. Child empowerment with a moral foundation.*

We were put in touch with the parents from a black family that had a few years of Steiner under their belts. The mother told us her kid said something astonishing to her in the car one day as they drove through a low-income neighborhood. Seeing grown men standing idly on a street corner in the middle of the day, the girl asked, "What would it take to help people realize their full potential?" It seems like such an innocent question until we try to answer it. The mom was reminded bitterly that, among the colleges that had accepted her when she was a high school senior, she'd chosen based on where her friends were going—Trenton State College over Cornell. We all have potential squandered for lack of information. In that sense I might argue that everyone *is* realizing their full potential. Perhaps potential is the wrong abstraction to apply.

Every choice is context specific, based on learned and conditioned behaviors, the examples of peers, the flukes of astronomical alignment at birth, structural forces arrayed to stabilize the balance of power and privilege in society, etcetera, etcetera. Instead of empowering folks to determine their own "full potential," those of us who have the wherewithal to make social critiques and assessments, myself included, project our potential onto others and decide when those others are either failing or unfairly more fortunate than ourselves. This is too

often the case whether we are talking about politics, education, or raising children.

The world as I know it will not be the world my children
will encounter. Not exactly. My job is to provide an environment where they'll feel safe and respected enough to develop
their imaginations inhibition-free. My job is to give them the
resources to realize the world they want to inherit—as long as
that world is founded on tolerance, respect, and a commitment
to social justice.

One website devoted to Steiner's pedagogy claimed Waldorf teachers "encourage what is hidden at the core of every
human being: the individual capable of exercising independence." Steiner dubbed this idiosyncratic approach to teaching "anthroposophy," emphasizing his intention to reveal core
wisdom (*sophia*) that, despite being hidden, he was convinced
is the essence of every human being (*anthropos*). Teaching, for
Steiner, does not consist of accumulating information. Rather,
he imagines it should liberate what is already present in children. In this, Steiner seems to have intuited at least some of
what is borne out by hard science. We now know, for instance,
that the brain develops in stages, so that it is of little use (and
may even be harmful) to *push* children, like forward-winding
so many clockwork toys. Steiner, unsurprisingly, was against
testing.

It would be as pointless to compare children with one
another developmentally as it would be to judge them on their
height or skull size. There is something totalitarian about our
obsession with standardized tests. Intentionally or not, assessment establishes a mean to which children are made to con-
form, which disregards, if not suppresses, their character. No
one person's understanding can precisely mirror another's.

W. B. Yeats, in his poem "Among School Children," asks, "O body swayed to music, O brightening glance, / How can we know the dancer from the dance?" Knowledge can't be isolated and measured independent of the child. There is no dance independent of the dancer.

Public school regulations often reduce learning to a kind of muscle memory, and reward children for how precisely they mirror their teachers' gestures. Steiner imagined a classroom where students grooved to the rhythms of their own bodies. Children would freely negotiate their own relationships to the material and, eventually, to society. This looks good on paper, but it might be naive in a society that receives some with openness and forbearance while it bullies others with shouts and contradictions.

In a place as segregated as New York City, I wonder if it might be irresponsible to practice the child-centered education Steiner advocated. Steiner's educational practice may be *intentionally* silent on the question of social identity, which sounds too much like the belief that if we stop talking about our socially constructed group differences they will go away. The poet Kyle Dargan draws a cogent analogy between race and climate change. We can stop talking about it, but that won't stop it from impacting people's lives. We like to think the problem with race is that we just need to be nicer to each other, but race is inscribed in our laws and institutions. I care more that my daughter has access to clean water and the resources necessary for her to make informed decisions than I care if a classmate of hers can tolerate her presence. Child-centered pedagogy has the tendency to disregard our "historical selves," as Claudia Rakine puts it, sharp-edged and hostile as these may be, and shroud them in ahistorical folklore and myths.

Could we afford to put the history, and therefore the explana-
tions, of economic and social inequality on the back burner?
And if so, for how long? There seems to be something essentially democratic about snowflake pedagogy, but if I shielded
my child from society as it had been organized by generations
before hers, would I be liberating her from the weight of history or simply declawing her?

   I noticed something when we visited the school, my dad said.
*I noticed there weren't any masks. Not one yin/yang symbol,
not one lizard, arabesque, or babushka. But there were plenty
of knights decorating the halls, plenty of fairies.* My father
pointed out how I'd painted myself into a corner. Any education in the humanities if not also math and science is grounded
in history and bound to *someone's* cultural frame—in this case
medieval Anglo-Saxon. And until I was ready to educate my
kids myself with the values unique to my social and historical
needs, I had to be willing, to some degree, to compromise. The
Rudyard Kipling poem "If," that anthem of relativity, came
to mind: "If you can dream—and not make dreams your master; / If you can think—and not make thoughts your aim . . ."
I tried to surrender to the paradox, so frustrated I almost burst
into song.

———

Rather than stew over the school's structural flaws, Ginger and
I attempted to compensate by getting active. We volunteered
at schoolwide events. I turned up at weekday coffee klatches
and morning knitting groups. We joined the Diversity Committee. The goals of the Diversity Committee were standard
fare: increase the number of families of color at the school,
broaden the cultural scope of the curriculum, and attract fac-

ulty of color. Working with the Diversity Committee made me more sympathetic to the challenges of diversifying institutions. In theory, there should have been no need for a Diversity Committee.

Diversity is the prize many independent schools are after, and yet that prize continues to be as elusive as ever. Many schools want to sport your child's nonthreatening nonwhite face on the banner of their home page—so long as your child and your family share the school's "dreams of the future." That is, so long as the family is reasonably suited to the culture of the school. Let's call it what is: tokenism, the appearance of progress without the growing pains. Programs like affirmative action and legacy admissions mostly piss off people who are not benefiting from them. Tokenism, however, makes everybody feel icky. But the alternative, laissez-faire approach feels irresponsible. All I'm sure about is that I don't give a shit how my kid gets into a good school. That's what I call a child-centered approach.

I've personally benefited from preferential policies. I know it. I have also been excluded from institutions for reasons having nothing to do with my preparation or ability. I understand the frustrations. Can you believe some schools give out scholarships for ultimate Frisbee? If I found out some ultimate Frisbee player got into a school that rejected me, I'd blame my misfortune on the Frisbee player. *I am more deserving than a damn Frisbee player.* The Frisbee player may be a concert violinist and speak four languages; all I'm going to focus on is the fact that he's a fucking Frisbee player.

But if a school were to offer my kid a scholarship for reasons other than her standardized test scores, I would not feel morally compromised by accepting that scholarship on behalf of my child. Do I imagine my descendants sitting around the pool house wringing their manicured hands over the question of whether or not their forebears were, at the time of their admission, underprepared for the schools they attended? Please. Will my progeny a hundred years hence weep with embarrassment over the hypothetical indignity that the flimsy notion of race factored into the dense algorithm used to determine their ancestor's suitability for some selective institution? If any of those future Pardlos do hang their heads in embarrassment, allow me to reanimate my cryogenically preserved corpse so I can smack them in their exquisitely orthodontured mouths.

Unfortunately, fear of a condescending side-eye from white families isn't the only deterrent for families of color considering schools like Steiner. Families of color and working-class and immigrant families often can't afford—I mean culturally—to let their kids develop "holistically." American families generally, but specifically those aspiring to the dominant culture, want measurable *proof* of their children's progress. They want their first-graders reciting the periodic table, building robots. Waldorf kids play in the woods. They build little houses out of sticks to shelter the homeless gnomes that have slipped through the social safety net of the forest. Waldorf kids don't encounter a textbook until third or fourth grade.

Even if families recognize that standardized tests are no better predictors of success than fortune cookies, and they are willing to trust in the organic development of their child, there is yet another deterrent. Waldorf pedagogy bans media and technology until the sixth grade, even in the home. No television, movies, video games, pads, pods, phones, or laptops. To enroll a kid in a Waldorf school is to commit the entire family to a nearly tech- and media-free lifestyle. Many parents cheat, of course, which isn't hard to figure out when teachers hear children in the stairwell singing songs from the latest Disney film. But one cannot participate in society and live off the media grid entirely.

Try kicking a media addiction when everything in the culture insists media is not only harmless, but also, like cigarettes back when people smoked in hospitals, healthy. Studies reveal that infants who are lulled to sleep each night by the white noise of a *Seinfeld* rerun are less likely to suffer from sleep disorders as adults. It is clinically proven that IMAX theaters, recalling the dream life of the womb, can mitigate the self-doubt and insecurity that accompanies the onset of puberty. Nine out of ten dermatologists agree that video games prevent children from touching their faces with greasy hands, thus lowering the incidence of pimples. I'm exaggerating, but people say the most outrageous things to defend their precious devices.

Ironically, Waldorf finds its most receptive market out west—the land of EST and experimental poetry, sure, but also of Hollywood and Silicon Valley. A 2011 article in *The New York Times* profiled the Waldorf school in Santa Clara County. According to Matt Richtel's "A Silicon Valley School That Doesn't Compute," Waldorf is popular among employees of the mammoth tech corporations precisely *because* of this ban on technology. The article then hyperlinks to another, earlier piece profiling a school district in Chandler, Arizona, that committed $33 million to outfitting classrooms with technology; standardized test scores in Chandler flatlined. This is affirmative proof of nothing, of course, but it is baseless to demonize the no-media policy.

"That school you put my granddaughter in is a cult," my father said, reacting to the no-media policy with confusion and horror. *Isn't that what the rating system is designed to do, warn you about movies that might give your kids bad ideas? What about animated films?* Finally, like a man reduced to bargaining for his life, he offered subterfuge: *It'll be our secret,* he'd say to the girls—as if we were maintaining our sensory diet under duress.

Our extended family, too, assumed there must be Kool-Aid involved. Tensions grew until my brother, Rob, having had our motives explained to him either third- or fourth-hand, decided to invoke his avuncular authority in my absence and attempt to save my culturally deprived children. The girls—mine: Sara and Fita; and his: Lyric—were visiting my mom for an evening. Rob, upon discovering Sara's unwillingness to watch television with Lyric, insisted that Sara sit in front of the tube. "In this house," he told her, "you're allowed." On the car ride home later, after I'd come to collect them, Sara began sniffling, clearly fighting tears as she allowed that Uncle Robbie made her watch television when she told him she wasn't allowed to. When I confronted my mother by phone, she defended my brother. "It's not like it was a snuff film," she said flatly. "It was friggin' Nickelodeon, for chrissakes."

Backhanded support came from the old man, who maintained that forcing Sara to watch television was unkind because she had already been "brainwashed." "That's not quite the right reasoning, Dad," I told him. "I'm trying to *keep* her from *becoming* brainwashed. But, regardless, you should respect our values no matter what's behind them. If we had converted to Islam, for example, would you force the child to eat pork just because you happen to have had a greasy, barbecued upbringing?"

"That's not 'quite the right' analogy," my father said, mocking me. "You can put pork in a container. You can subtract it from your life. Media, though, that's everywhere—like the *smell* of pork. Only way you're going to avoid odors, hell, is to stop breathing."

"No, but we can *limit* it," I chimed, attempting to quell the tension with song. One point for team Steiner.

"Limit or replace?" he asked, his tone wagging a finger. "However much you might reduce it, that space is gonna be filled with something else. They're teaching kids their version of how the world works, all right. They just aren't using technology to do it. 'Cause these messages are still all around us, within us. The point isn't to keep the kids' minds open to the wonders of their own creative genius. If that were the case, we would applaud the Chinese government for 'protecting' the minds of its citizens. Waldorf just *postpones* exposure to television and computers so nothing will disrupt their *own* brand of social programming."

My father ended this brief polemic by coughing the word "cult." I saw his point. Only I had decided that, cult or no cult, it feels good being a part of something. It feels good knowing that across the world there are families upholding the same values as ours. It feels good knowing my kids are happy and safe. That should be enough. Why should I be defensive? The best schools tend to be a little cultish. What is education if not mass socialization?

———

"Whoa, whoa, whoa, your kids can't go down there," the security guard called to us, having tracked us from the auditorium of Intermediate School 383. We were venturing toward the empty corridor, and the girls had taken off running into its dark maw.

Ginger was an alum of the school, she explained, and had in fact been valedictorian in the early eighties. She just wanted to show her family "really quick. My name is on the plaque down there."

"Ma'am, you can't just walk up in here," the guard replied. "This is a secure area, all right? Gotta be cleared first."

Ginger let out an irritated sigh. "What harm can you possibly think I'm going to do?"

"Lady, all I can tell you is you gotta go to the office." The door she pointed toward was a short way down the hall. "Right where that lady's going in, see?"

The lady in question was the vice principal Ginger had spoken to when setting up the event, the person who'd finally returned her call. Ginger proceeded to explain the situation to the vice principal, who seemed confused. She wanted to accommodate us—the parents had raved about just how helpful and informative Ginger's presentation was—but couldn't imagine what it was Ginger was trying to describe. "You mean some kind of trophy?" Flummoxed, she let Ginger lead us to the place where we might find the blessed memorial. All we found was a blank wall, its only occupant a hand-sanitizing dispenser. Ginger seemed somehow prepared for the loss. Standing there before our own sense of anticlimax, we didn't notice Sara walking a little farther down along the hallway, on into the grim twilight of a lone fire emergency light.

Sara called back to us from the gloom. And there it was: "The General Thaddeus Kosciuszko Award for Scholarship, Character and Service." The plaque listed twenty-seven names in two columns beginning with "Yoreel Johnson, 1967." We found, two-thirds of the way down the left column, "Ginger Romero, 1979." The twenty-six-year tradition of emblazoning the names of exceptional students ended in 1993, which made the plaque seem a little like Charlie Brown's Christmas tree, a fleeting memorial bookended by eras of hope and apathy. But that didn't stop us from cheering in vindication. The bronze lettering glinting in the glow of the guard's flashlight was proof that Ginger, and by extension all of us, belonged here. I wondered what became of the twenty-six other people whose names were inscribed on the plaque. Those names, the lives they represented, were as mysterious as the lives waiting down the long corridor of the future before my children.

Tolle, Lege

For generations, or so I've heard, Brooklyn families have shrugged off the city swelter, crowding I-87 North en route to the Catskills for summer weekends. In July 2016, partly in search of traditions that might bind our family to a community, Ginger and I joined the exodus. It was our second annual hauling of the Volvo, overstuffed like a circus wagon with a hodgepodge of duffels and rolly bags, and our two girls, Sara and Fita, who fought over holding Oliver, the family rabbit. With a generic soul singer—the voice we downloaded for the GPS—as our field guide, we avoided the highway and bushwhacked the rural roads to the temperate oasis of Fleischmanns, a small town seasonally occupied by Orthodox Jews. We were gentiles—outsiders, as the word implies, a role we found comfortably familiar.

This was my first family trip as the undisputed elder Pardlo male. Even after his death, and even though what contact I had with my father in the previous five years was mostly in texts and rare phone calls by which I recognized him, figuratively and literally, as "unavailable" on my caller ID, I was still competing with him. In the end, he was convinced I hated him, which wasn't true, but he'd become so delusional by then I couldn't tell if he was high or merely unhinged. I couldn't tell his heartfelt self-pity from manipulation. The reality that he was gone, that our cold war was finally over, left a deficit of purpose in my life.

Alan, Cynthia, and their two kids lived in the Catskills the entire season, in a house owned by the synagogue where Cynthia served as rabbi, which, considering the town population maxed out in the double digits during the off-season, made them locals. We were there for the card games and camaraderie, and to scavenge used bookstores for the weekend. We so anticipated the trip that it had the aura of a family reunion. We jokingly considered printing matching T-shirts for everyone to mark the occasion.

On the first day, Alan took the kids out for ice cream and found a local bookshop on the way, where he scored a complete set of the *Boys' and Girls' Bookshelf,* a ten-volume set of books from 1912. The subtitle was *A Practical Plan of Character Building.* It looked like a precursor to the *World Book Encyclopedia* set, those books that entertained me as a kid when there was nothing on television. Unlike the *World Book,* however, the *Bookshelf* wasn't alphabetized. It was organized by topic, with titles like "True Stories from Every Land" and "Wonders of Invention." When we came across a spread on the building of the *Titanic,* Alan palmed his forehead: the *Titanic* hadn't sunk yet.

As Alan put one volume back and grabbed another, I shuffled between the dusty covers in my lap: anthropologists at work. The books implied hilariously rigid gender norms, but we also learned that, in 1912, it seems there were three distinct races of humans on earth: Negroid, Caucasoid, and Mongoloid. Also, the planet was stocked with unlimited resources begging to be exploited. Asia consisted of China and Japan, and the people who lived there were all called "Chinamen." Less surprisingly, Indians were noble and, not to mention, fun to imitate in speech and dress.

I figured the average black person in 1912 must have had to deal with pretty shitty conditions in public life, and these books targeted middle-class white American families who would have interacted with blacks while they were in uniform as domestic servants, barbers, train porters, caterers: occupations obscured from view by strict codes of conduct. The *Bookshelf* probably wouldn't detail the structural and political shittiness surrounding black people's public lives, I expected, but it must have *something* to say on race in America. They couldn't have ignored the existence of black people altogether, right?

There was a small section on the games played by "Negro boys and girls." Alan and I riffled through the index. Uhm, how about slavery? What did it have to say about slavery? Bupkis. Unless you count the Fugitive Slave Act appearing on a timeline of notable legislation. Also, the books noted, slavery may have been a factor in the Civil War.

Say what you will, but 1912 wasn't *that* long ago in the life span of cultural memory. A century in the life of a nation is like twenty years in the life of an individual. Segregation, train tracks, redlining, and generational cycles of class alienation: these combined could isolate a white family so completely from the shared social memory we call history as to cultivate a naive conviction in the impartiality of justice and economic opportunity in America.

"Blind spots," my new buzzword, replaces "microaggressions" in my vocabulary. Microaggressions are aggressive if we understand them from the perspective of the recipient alone. If, on the other hand, we identify, for the moment, with the alleged aggressor, we might see the interaction differently, and negotiate it with fewer fucks given. There is a danger of blaming the victim in this, but if I know the aggression is coming, either I can be butt-hurt about it and suffer or I can prepare for it, and engage it in a way that creates the possibility of an outcome I can live with. It's like defensive driving: I might have the right of way, but I'd rather avoid the old coot barreling in from the merging lane than spend two hours on the shoulder explaining to an indifferent cop how the only other vehicle on the road clipped my passenger-side mirror. Indeed, all anyone can do with microaggressions is either point a finger or apologize. On the other hand, hunting and cracking open blind spots as if they were Easter eggs is something fun we can all do together. There are too many people who consider themselves white and are absolutely dear to me. My friendships with them are life-sustaining, but they are nonetheless capable of saying some really dumb shit. And so am I, which is why I am convinced this is not a question of will.

Garden-variety microaggressions are involuntary, inadvertent, the result of ignorance and classical conditioning, and usually find sanctuary in blind spots. I want Americans to be united in the commitment to routinely interrogate our individual relationships to the narratives that shape our national identity—to abhor blind spots that derail our pursuit of social justice. Perhaps this just means that one day we'll all share the same blind spots, a harmonious choir of blinkered thinking, but then, what more than this is the definition of a community?

I want to start from scratch, I told Alan and Cynthia the next morning over breakfast. I want to reinvent America. I want to forgive us our history of slavery, and the crackpot invention of race we've used first to maintain that peculiar institution, and then later to designate an exploitable surplus population. And let's forgive the debt, too; it would be impossible to administer reparations anyway, and to whom would we make financial amends? The day the government announced it was giving reparations for slavery, there would be such an overwhelming acknowledgment of African ancestry that Americans of all hues would crash the servers at the Census Bureau declaring their precious one drop of blackness. What I'm after is something more valuable than a government check.

In our new America, each July Fourth we will celebrate freedom *and* our ongoing struggle to defeat selfish and tyrannical impulses in every one of our American hearts. Each Thanksgiving, in addition to our thanks for the sacrifices of Native Americans, and for the Pilgrims' travails, we will give thanks for the sacrifices of all those who gave freely, if not willfully, their bodies' labor to produce the national nest egg of wealth we have since hatched and grown into a global juggernaut. Every Memorial Day, in addition to honoring known and unknown soldiers (including the many Revolutionary War veterans whose pensions were withheld because they were black), we will honor all those who risked their lives, and those heroes who gave their lives escaping and/or defeating slavery. We will revel in the richness of our diversity, we will celebrate the epic collusion of American culture. For Columbus Day, we will reach across the Americas to remember the voyages that enriched the nascent West: *La Niña, La Pinta, La Santa Maria, La Amistad,* the *Clotilde,* the *Wanderer,* the *Hope* (to name a few of the most legendary slave ships), and the *Mayflower.*

"Good luck with that," said Alan.

I admit it is idealistic. Some might say we're more likely to convince Congress to grant reparations. But I'm committing this book to the dream of a new America.

———

"If a man has not discovered something that he will die for, he isn't fit to live." So resounded MLK's maxim in my childhood home, pitching family life at the highest intensity level, no matter the adversity. I was twelve when I joined my father in the commitment that scarred his character and shaped mine. It appeared to me then, and I know it to be true now, that the air traffic control strike of 1981 was the defining moment in my father's life. A pivotal point for me by proxy; the strike still shapes how I understand all that happened before and after it in my life. My father was fond of reciting from memory the Rudyard Kipling poem "If":

If

If you can keep your head when all about you
  Are losing theirs and blaming it on you,
If you can trust yourself when all men doubt you,
  But make allowance for their doubting too;
If you can wait and not be tired by waiting,
  Or being lied about, don't deal in lies,
Or being hated, don't give way to hating,
  And yet don't look too good, nor talk too wise:

If you can dream—and not make dreams your master;
*   If you can think—and not make thoughts your aim;*
If you can meet with Triumph and Disaster
*   And treat those two impostors just the same;*
If you can bear to hear the truth you've spoken
*   Twisted by knaves to make a trap for fools,*
Or watch the things you gave your life to, broken,
*   And stoop and build 'em up with worn-out tools:*

If you can make one heap of all your winnings
*   And risk it on one turn of pitch-and-toss,*
And lose, and start again at your beginnings
*   And never breathe a word about your loss;*
If you can force your heart and nerve and sinew
*   To serve your turn long after they are gone,*
And so hold on when there is nothing in you
*   Except the Will which says to them: "Hold on!"*

If you can talk with crowds and keep your virtue,
*   Or walk with Kings—nor lose the common touch,*
If neither foes nor loving friends can hurt you,
*   If all men count with you, but none too much;*
If you can fill the unforgiving minute
*   With sixty seconds' worth of distance run,*
Yours is the Earth and everything that's in it,
*   And—which is more—you'll be a Man, my son!*

———

If I'm not willing to *die* for my dream of a new America, I am at least willing to be reckless for it. To recall the Kipling poem in my father's voice is to clear a path through the debris of self-doubt, if only long enough to move my life a few metaphorical steps in the direction of my American Dream.

I am a poet. Poetry and civic duty share a porous border in my mind. Being a poet doesn't make me virtuous. Poetry never prevented me from totaling a car. No shrink wrote me a prescription for poetry. Poetry never represented me in court. Poems can't keep me from getting mugged or roughed up by police. Poetry never cured a hangover, and it never paid a bar tab. Although I have wept and prayed to poetry to ease my burden in these and other regards, which have constituted, at one time or another, the core preoccupations of my daily life, poetry answers no prayers. Poetry is useless to me in all but one way. Reading it makes me a nicer person.

Reading poetry has improved my ability to intuit, and thereby negotiate more effectively, the needs and desires of others. I'm no mind reader, but poetry puts me in tune with the unarticulated registers of language, a skill that, through reflection, also helps me identify my own blind spots. The best poems model the kind of work I want to do on myself. It's difficult to identify my strengths and flaws on my own, especially if I've spent my life around people who think, act, and perceive the world in the same way that I do. Especially in diversity-poor environments, poetry is the best supplement to help getting out of one's own head.

Poetry teaches me this because in order to "get" a poem, you need to find its fulcrum, a tipping point that is rarely obvious. Most poems have a moment when something shifts. It may be midway through or at the end. This is the moment of transformation—we call it a *volta,* or "turn." The turn could be a plot twist or a change in tone. You can identify the turn by comprehending first the poem's overall patterns and prevailing logic. There might be many patterns in a single poem, and some or all of them might get broken or disrupted over its course, but the *volta* is special in that it marks the moment when the poem breaks its deepest and most characteristic habit. There is rarely a single turn that everyone can agree on, and who cares if everyone agrees. Reading is a solitary exercise, a union of one. The detective work of looking for the *volta* is what gets us into the poem, makes us rewrite the poem in our own voice and consciousness.

For example, I've spent hours working out when Gwendolyn Brooks, in her 1963 poem "The Lovers of the Poor," first signals that the "Ladies from the Ladies' Betterment League" are going to hightail it out of the tenement house they are prospecting for their charity. Is it when the smells of the tenement begin to vex them?

> But it's all so bad! and entirely too much for them.
> The stench; the urine, cabbage, and dead beans,
> Dead porridges of assorted dusty grains,
> The old smoke, heavy diapers, and, they're told,
> Something called chitterlings.

Or when they look in horror at the emblem of poverty made by the woman and her children in a doorway? Is it when they see the rat? I'm inclined to identify with the "Ladies" (and I think Brooks wants me to), because I can see how they've misread their relationship to their own power and privilege, and how that misreading of self comes most sharply into focus against the unfamiliar (to the Ladies) background of the tenement house.

Some poetry lovers claim that poems don't have to have a

turn. This is usually what people say in defense of shitty poems. *Of course* there has to be a transformative moment, a moment in which we experience not just the characters or speaker in the poem, but the poet herself in crisis. The turn doesn't have to bring the reader to any grand epiphany or catharsis, but if—whether I'm writing the poem or reading it—I walk away from the poem without feeling like I've just survived a vicarious encounter with some unqualified measure of intensity that I could not have created on my own, if I feel like the placid surface of my consciousness has suffered not so much as a ripple, then I'd say that poem owed me an apology for having wasted my time. If there is no turn, no transformative moment, then the poem is a journal entry, at best a laundry list of reflections and anecdotes, or what I think of as a "litany of relapses"— the barren passage of time unthwarted, moving predictably toward a predictable end. "The moment of change is the only poem," says Adrienne Rich.*

If nothing is risked, if nothing is offered in sacrifice, then there is nothing to draw poet and reader together. Without risk, the reader has no reason, other than being nosy, to be invested. Without risk, the poem is a screen rather than a medium. It's a visit to the zoo. We want access, vulnerability, flesh. Isaac did not literally have to die. God, lacking poetry, wanted to feel Abraham's devotion was *real*. The poem is a ritual space for the *practice* of feeling.

There is no feeling in monotony. We have to establish something before and something after. The teacher M. Degas in Philip Levine's poem "M. Degas Teaches Art & Science at Durfee Intermediate School, Detroit 1942" draws a line on the

* I'm being harsh, I know. There are many conceptual poems that produce a productive disturbance in the mind. I don't mean to dismiss turn-less poetry out of hand.

chalkboard and asks his students to describe what he has just done. The poem turns when the brightest student in the class replies, "You have begun to separate the dark from the dark." This is one of the most fundamental justifications for art I can think of: the moment of change is the only poem.

Behind the Wheel

No one has offered any suggestions, and the car—my mother-in-law in the backseat between the girls—feels fuller than normal. I've taken charge and made an executive decision. It's Mother's Day. I decided there was no need to prepare this Get-Along Gang for where we are going by informing them of our destination. And yet my wife, Ginger, asks why I am taking DeKalb when it always clogs up where they put in the new bike lanes. She thinks she knows where I'm going. Because it is a nearly room temperature evening, she thinks I must want to find a sidewalk café in Fort Greene where we can sit and be seen and people-watch. So she thinks. And, OK, she's right—I do. But I don't want her to *know* she is right, so now I have to think of something else.

"Would have been faster to keep going down Marcy to Myrtle," Ginger says, facing her window.

Fita considers her car seat more of a recliner than an eggcup and uses the shoulders of Ginger's seat in front of her as an ottoman. Sara, at seven, already affecting a preteen ennui, leans forward on her booster as if it were the perch on a dunk tank. *Let's get this over with,* her attitude seems to say. Granny sits between them, prim as a governess. I am driving through Bed-Stuy, with its intermittent construction sites dotting the landscape like those first fat little grapes of rain on a windshield. The neighborhood is "in transition," we say, as is often said of the dying. Each year more people walking dogs, more people riding skateboards. Fewer and fewer police helicopters with klieg lights searching the ground like UFO abduction beams. More and more yellow cabs (as opposed to the green cabs native to Brooklyn and Queens) conducting their only licit business this side of the East River: dropping off fares from Manhattan. We've spent the day at the Brooklyn Botanical Garden, but the weather is so nice no one's ready to go home.

"Why do you always give traffic advice in the conditional past tense?" I say. "It's like you wait until I do something so you can call it a mistake. You know what would have been faster? It *would have* been faster if we all had jet packs. It *would have* been faster if we had stayed home." Ginger dismisses me, turning that invisible key in the lock that seals her lips, and tossing it clear out the window.

In response to some complaint I must not have heard, Fita bites into the wet flesh of an apple Granny's produced from her purse. We are passing a tent revival being held in a vacant lot annexed by the adjacent church, and the music is lively but, it seems to me, unreasonably loud. Nevertheless, I slow the car for effect, making use of the fortuitous soundtrack outside.

"What's that," Fita asks through a mouthful of apple.

"That's a church," I say.

Sara says it is *not* and argues that in church people sit around listening to boring poems.

"I don't like this apple," says Fita. "The meat inside's too furry."

"They're not poems, Sara. They're called sermons, which I *guess* are kind of like poems," I say, thinking about Walt Whitman and James Weldon Johnson and how they often imitated preachers in their poems. "And not all churches do the same things anyway."

Abruptly, I am interrupted by the radio. Ginger doesn't like it when I talk about churches or religion. She thinks I'm disrespectful. She fiddles with the radio a moment more to make sure this line of query is stymied before it grows. She doesn't want me provoking her mother. I know this. I know what she's thinking. I wait until Ginger finds a volume equivalent to plugging her fingers in her ears and singing *lalalalala*.

"This church is the kind where people like to sing," I say, over an NPR story about the health risks of circumcision, angling my voice higher to compete with Brian Lehrer, the radio announcer.

"That man sounds like he has a cold," says Fita who only wants to eat the skin now.

"The man on the radio?"

"No, that other man, the one who keeps clearing his throat."

"That's the preacher, and that's the way people *want* him to sound," I say.

"Why do people go to church?" Sara asks, finally. At this, Ginger, whose cousins called her Mother Superior when she was a kid, drops her chin to her chest.

It has been a sore point with Ginger that we don't go to church. Not that she is particularly observant, but the lapse is one more reminder of the distance she has drifted from her Salvadoran roots. It means something to her, the ritual that is Catholicism. And it troubles her, too, that the average white kid on the Upper East Side being raised by a Latin American nanny may be more familiar with Latino culture than her own two children. It didn't help that Sara recently asked why Christians get what she called "angry" whenever they see a "plus sign."

In the roller derby of this conversation, Ginger has been adjusting her straps, fitting her helmet. Now she's ready to step onto the track to body check us all off course, and with the first impulsively thrown elbow she asks me, "Are *you* circumcised?"

You got to hand it to her.

Fita wants to know why apples can be yellow and still we call them apples.

"People go to church in order to be with others who think about the world in the same way they do," I tell Sara.

Then Sara asks, "How come we don't go to church?"

"Can't believe I asked that," Ginger says in a rhetorical snort, and then conspiratorially: "I mean, that's something I should know, right?"

"We do go to a place like that," I tell Sara. "Only we don't call it church. We call it the coffee shop." In the welter, in the rearview mirror, I notice Granny chuckling devilishly. My soundtrack slowly fading as I address the imaginary fourth wall, the audience of brownstones reeling by on my left, I announce: *This is my marriage in a nutshell.*

"Los cipotes tienen hambre," says Granny, as if merely to add texture, two cents. I'm convinced Granny revels in discord and havoc, secretly at home in the briar patch. What better Mother's Day, then, for my mother-in-law?

"Apples don't have to look the same to be related, Fita. Look at us," Sara says. Then Sara asks if all people in the world are related and we're just such a big family that we've all forgotten how.

We approach an intersection where a new apartment building has replaced a junkyard. Half clad in glass and burnished sheets of aluminum, the building is obscured along the sidewalk by blue construction walls. There is a parade-float-sized inflatable rat that the girls notice simultaneously, if their screams are any indication. The screams are only for effect, though. By now they are perfectly familiar with the rat, having seen it at several construction sites around Brooklyn where developers aren't using union labor. Before I have the chance to explain, the girls conjecture this moveable protest is a mascot, some invitation to play, the way it visually rhymes with the bouncy houses people rent for block parties.

"What's the difference between a rat and a scab again?" Sara asks.

"There is no difference. It's just that no one will get the idea if protesters put up a giant inflatable wound. But for your information it's somebody who doesn't belong to a union doing a job that should be done by someone who *does* belong to a union."

"*What's* a union again?"

"It's like—" I'm struggling on this one, but I'm a good dad, I try to give the answers. "It's like the people who belong to a church." Ginger cuts her eyes at me. Bad idea. Better idea: "Or a classroom. Like *your* class. And it's like if it is your turn to draw the week's nature scene for the room's bulletin board and Mrs. Kelly decides at the last minute she wants somebody else to do it because this other person, I don't know, does it faster or uses fewer crayons or something. That person should say,

'I'm sorry, Mrs. Kelly, but it's Sara's turn to draw a picture for the class.' That person should say, 'If you put me on the schedule, Mrs. Kelly, I'll be happy to draw a picture when it's my turn.' But what if the classmate doesn't say that? And instead she goes ahead and puts up her own picture when she knows good and well it ain't her turn? That would make her a scab, and you and your classmates should take her to the rooftop and beat her with a sack of oranges." I don't actually say this last part, but the image, a vestige of my father's humor, darts bat-like through my mind. "A scab is someone who does her own thing instead of sticking together with everyone else," I say, finally.

An ellipsis hangs in the air, though it's not yet clear whether this is the silence of a point well conveyed or the opposite.

"But isn't that what we're *supposed* to do?" Sara asks.

The Strip

He was already stubbing out his cigarette in the planter as I hooked the Econoline van around to meet him under the carport of the Willow Grove Hampton Inn. His hair was still wavy, I could see, kind of Latin, and raked with silver. It had been so long since I last saw him, I wasn't sure whether he was still straightening it or if the follicles had simply wilted with age. Not many years before this, he was routinely mistaken for the plump, middle-aged Al Sharpton; I wondered if people also mistook him for the caved-in, pencil-necked person Sharpton became. He was thin, my dad, as if he ought to be sporting a walking staff and dhoti. This shocked me. I wanted it to be a trick of the light, and as I squinted and craned my head forward, I clipped the curb, causing the empty van to buck and then rumble like an oil drum. Getting in, he groaned as he pulled himself up with the handle above the doorframe. "The worst part is the loss of strength," he said without even commenting on my driving, though his fingers remained wrapped around the handle above him once he was securely in. The veins in his wrist were big as soft-drink straws, and I could make out the bulge of the shunt peeking from where his silk shirt and leather jacket sleeves bunched down past his elbow on the raised arm. His clothes were sized for a much larger man than this new father of mine.

It had been almost two years since his near-fatal kidney failure. That failure—occurring not long after my parents' separation—resulted from sustained attempts to regulate his blood sugar with Mountain Dew and Thin Mints. He'd only recently begun submitting to regular dialysis treatment, surrendering his freedom for twelve hours a week. Suffice it to say he was reluctant, half hoping intervention from the eternal footman might render the matter moot.

I wanted to say something about global warming, why we could wear jackets in the middle of February instead of proper coats, but I didn't want to provoke a rant about hopelessness and the world's end. *Just look at the damn space program,* he'd offer in a Miles Davis rasp in our most recent phone calls. The Shuttle *Atlantis,* like a mote of jeweler's dust, had barely scratched the atmosphere on reentry and touched down at Kennedy Space Center before NASA workers were packing up the booms and rigging of the entire program. Folding the lion cages. Rolling up the tent. A sign, my father said, that mankind would never again breach the heavens in search of the forbidden absolute. A sign that we'd given up and that there wouldn't be a generation like his again for some time to come, if ever. Sensing his mortality, he wanted to synchronize his life with historic events. He imagined himself a rare species of comet; he scanned newspapers for hard proof of the providential timing of his exit.

He kept a pair of pliers on the kitchen counter at his place in Vegas. He said it was the only way he could open anything with a twist top. I allowed myself to picture what his kitchen might look like by collaging descriptions he'd given me with what I knew of my father's lifestyle and impatience for decorating. I pictured counters littered with a bachelor's corkscrew, toaster oven, coffeemaker. Pliers. And then, some kind of reclining chair in the living room centered on a plasma TV just beyond the breakfast bar, sunlight slipping under a window shade like a hotel bill. Perhaps my father made an awkward attempt to personalize the furnished space with a framed poster of Worf, his favorite *Star Trek* character, he would have purchased from some tourist shop around the corner. Alone, he would have been even less circumspect about the Ziploc baggies and amber glass vials emptied of blow and strewn across the glass top of a faux wicker coffee table.

Did he have pictures of his family? Ginger and I had once given him an electronic picture frame loaded with a dozen digital photos of us. There was Sara building little houses out of twigs in the park; and there was Ginger, fake-freckled in a Pippi Longstocking costume, holding Fita the fluffy green dinosaur with her plastic pumpkin container for trick-or-treating; and there I was at a podium, reading before an audience at the Brooklyn Public Library.

He claimed he didn't "get" poetry. In sports, you know who's the best, right? It's the guy who crosses the finish line first, the guy left standing over the crumpled body of his opponent. Poetry, my dad said, is like a game at a children's birthday party. What's the point if everybody wins? Writing is its own reward I've explained to him many times, but I couldn't help wishing I was raising a Super Bowl trophy over my head in that photo.

I told myself he liked the picture frame. Back in Willow Grove, it was propped beside his chair, on the shelf that doubled as a TV table, offering glimpses of the future illumined through the haze of cigarette smoke and cat hair.

"Why Vegas?" I asked him finally. I looked over to where he sat in the passenger seat. He ticked off each finger like light switches: *a view of the strip; a culture of moral relativism; the best emergency response times in the country; a devastated housing market; legal prostitution.* Then, baring his palms as if in supplication to rest his case, the weight of his argument almost too much to hold: *and oyster bars.*

"You can find a town with a better reputation for seafood, you know. Entire cultures, even."

"I'm not you," he said, before adding, "I don't like foreigners in *my* country; why would I bother with them in theirs?"

I'd heard variations of this list before. None of the reasons had ever been satisfying to me. The one item in each recitation that had a shiver of living truth—like a spotted banana in an arrangement of plastic fruit—was that "view of the strip." He was in Vegas awhile before I realized what that must have meant to him, all those years later, the view, a tower rising out the desert, a landscape so much like Oklahoma. In images of Vegas I pulled up on the web, the strip looked like an airport runway at night, edge lights along the boulevard narrowing to an arrowhead aimed at the dark flank of the mountain.

"I heard you found some kind of high-tech Jiffy Lube," I said as I pulled out onto the main road.

He chuckled. "Looks like a damn massage parlor. The last place, I swear they used cheesecloth to filter my blood. Took days." A beat. "But *this* place?—in and out." And then a sigh. "For my kidney to be pecked out again another day."

Easton Road snaked to the right after braiding once with

York Road through big box stores and restaurant chains. We followed the bend around Toys "R" Us.

"I talked to Mommy," I said.

"Sounds like it," he answered. I tried to be patient, to separate the man who was my father from the guy who owed my mother alimony. "Dragging my ass up and down the turnpike like Sparky. For what?" I didn't turn to look at him. I didn't have to. I could sense his expectant eyes on me. *Sparky.* In tribute and reflex, I responded silently: *What do you call a dog with no hind legs and steel balls?* His pause was calculated to give me time to process his subtle wit, which was more important than his indignation for having been made to commute "up and down the turnpike" for so many years. "You know how bad she jacked me in the divorce? Huhn? I mean, where am I supposed to get all this money she's asking for? She doesn't get to hold my life hostage."

"What about the car?" It was a Mercedes. A two-seater convertible. Silver, with burgundy interior.

"The car," he puffed, waving the air as if I was a bug he was forced to swat from his face. "I know you've got some *thing* against the car." He leaned over as if about to show me the secret to whistling through my fingers. "And it's not even that you really want me to give your mother a piece of the car, *is* it? You just don't want *me* to have it."

It was true. I failed to see what a senior citizen on dialysis and a fixed income could need with a sixty-thousand-dollar sports car. It was wasteful and stupid. "Doesn't matter what I think about the car, Dad. Just that in the world the rest of us live in, you can't fucking afford it."

We were headed to the storage facility to collect the stuff

he didn't ship before driving "the car" from Willow Grove to Vegas. He had stopped paying the mortgage he'd taken out on Willow Grove, and my mother moved back to Tinker Place, which was quieter now that City High had broken up and Robbie was trying to get sober. My dad had hired someone to move his remaining items into a storage facility before the bank boarded up that house. He couldn't afford storage any longer. Some of those things would be going to my house in Brooklyn. Others he would pack up to take on the plane with him back to Vegas.

"Look, I'm not going to defend the car. All right? I earned it. I deserve it. She gets to have her gray-haired prom, right? So now it's *my* turn to squish my toes in the ice cream."

"You're keeping the car out of spite, Dad, and you know it—not because you're actually getting any enjoyment out of it. You're like Sara, stuffing the last few cookies into her mouth just so her sister won't get any."

"For hate's sake," he growled, "I spit my last breath at thee." He was quoting Khan. I might have told him that Khan was quoting Ahab, but why bother.

We idled in the middle of the intersection, holding traffic as I waited to turn into the lot. The turn signal was ticking. What I did know was that "the car" was the last sentimental keepsake of his former life, the life in which he enjoyed social ties and family relations. What I didn't know yet, what would come as no surprise, was that my father was careening down the steep side of an opiate addiction. He escaped to Vegas to be free of oversight and the stifling care of loved ones.

His move marked the first time my dad lived outside of the Delaware Valley. It was a regression, a return to the traumatic moment of departure from the glorious future his adolescence heralded.

I imagined he was a rising high school junior debating the merits of his reach school. He would choose UNLV because it was in Vegas, and he'd choose Vegas because Disneyland had neither a university nor naked ladies. Vegas spun illusions out of the surplus of life's unyielding truths. My dad was impatient with the limits of truth. This thought exercise allowed me to meet my father as a peer and a friend, and the beginning of that promising friendship made the most fitting end to the story we shared.

On *Intervention*

Rather than a private, homebound affair, our intervention was broadcast worldwide on the Emmy-award-winning reality cable TV show. My mother strong-armed me into being on *Intervention* because, she insisted, Robbie's drinking, as of the fall of 2009, had hit rock bottom. The show promised to give us all the tools and support we needed to surround Robbie with tough love, force him to answer for the destruction his drinking had caused, and secure his commitment to repair his section of the emotional network that we had created as a family. Cameras would record the operation from multiple angles. I had seen a few episodes of the show on the A&E channel. Lives dragged by galloping addictions, the enablers routinely stitching together excuses in the pattern of their own nostalgic fantasies, the head-on collisions of fever dream and court-mandated recovery, and the occasional new sprig of life emerging from ashes of redemption: I can't say I was a fan, but I watched it now and then. I watched it enough to know that it seemed kosher in the abstract, when the family profiled was not my own. The idea that mine might be one of those families was galling.

My mother was willing to leverage my mental health to stabilize Robbie's devastated self-worth and, after the initial airing, make the spectacle available for download from Amazon.com for $1.99. She knew I had a drinking problem. *How are you going to invite an alcoholic to intervene on another alcoholic?* I asked her. *It don't make no sense.* I thought the endeavor was a waste of time. Robbie would see this intervention had no teeth. We may as well have threatened to rat him out to Santa. Alcoholics are crafty—whether in spite of or because of the ramparts of denial they raise to protect their destructive enterprises. Both of my mother's parents were alcoholics. My grandmother had been sober for decades, but my grandfather Bob still drank. Alcoholism was the Muzak of our familial dysfunction. Most of the time, we didn't even notice it.

No one would dispute that after six DUIs, Robbie was a danger to himself and others, but I suspect (whether my suspicion is fair or not is a risk I'm willing to take) this danger wasn't my mother's sole motivation. When I asked her why she arranged for us all to be on *Intervention,* she explained bitterly, "My son was a successful musician, and had become a falling down, belligerent drunk." She thought he was an embarrassment, but there was no question in her mind that Robbie was sick and in need of her rescue. It would have been callous—even for me—to suggest, in 2008, that he should have been delivered to the criminal justice system for a more spartan state-sponsored rehabilitation program.

I didn't want to play a role in the television show or any other serial drama that ends each week on a cliffhanger. *What new life-threatening slapstick adventure does Robbie's drinking have in store for him? Tune in next week to find out!!* Keep a safe distance, and let Robbie's disease run its course, was what

I thought. Love is a shabby deterrent to drinking, anyway. I never met an alcoholic who stopped drinking against his will. The best we can do from the outside is have faith that the alcoholic has somewhere inside him a survival gene that will kick in at some intolerable point of depravity. Walk away, Mom, it's none of your business, I told her. He's a grown-ass man.

She'd tried "everything." I know she'd signed Robbie up for free counseling sessions at the Catholic Charities. She made me come down to New Jersey from New York to join in. She considered treatment centers and clinics as doorsteps to which she could deliver—like a babe in a wicker basket—her adult son for care. She finally reached out to the producers of *Intervention* in the hopes that they could help Robbie where so many others had failed, she told me. Failed *her,* I would add.

My mother intuited the singularly most productive gesture that would set the machinery of our lives ratcheting toward her desired outcome. With the one deft e-mail she posted to the show's website, she appealed to an authority that could facilitate, witness, and record Robbie's transformation, prove her maternal mettle and our family's cohesion, and reassert our narrative of exceptionalism. "There's no such thing as bad publicity," my father would remind us, along with "Never let a good crisis go to waste." Why should it matter if, at the same time, she helped Robbie stop drinking?

She told me that when Robbie was a kid, she decided she "wasn't going to let the world chew him up like every other black boy." I accused her of being more concerned for Robbie's career than his health. Like a Mafia don who pretends infirmity to deflect attention, she responded, "If only I were that sophisticated." She claimed naiveté so often that my father used to call her Jiminy Cricket.

The show's producers portrayed her as a mother in denial, self-deceived, a common enabler. She could hide the truth in the baldest statements. "I never thought, at thirty, Robbie would be here," she told the camera. "You never would have made me believe this. Never." This was true, and she would go on refusing to accept that Robbie was capable of astounding self-sabotage.

———

Intervention had its participants, with the help of a professional social worker, counselor, or therapist serving as the "interventionist," unite with their families, in some cases for the first time in years. The families demand that their troubled loved-one commit to treatment for her or his addiction or else "there will be consequences." The producers' intention (as I was reassured, and had no reason to doubt) was to show how addiction cuts across class, race, and religion, across histories and politics—as powerfully universal as the love it tests. Screening for the show would begin on the website, where applicants were invited to submit personal narratives outlining the toxic loved one's faults and failures. How many people had the wherewithal, patience, and writing skills needed to compose these personal narratives? This step alone must have weeded out the majority of families in demographics that are statistically most vulnerable to alcohol and substance abuse. Without a story, an alcoholic is a statistic. And a statistic isn't sympathetic.

Neither is there suspense in a story where Mommy and Daddy are certain, as always, to scoop up the wreckage left by a wayward child with platinum credit cards for dustpans. Unless the wayward child comes off like Patty Duke in *The*

Miracle Worker or Linda Blair in *The Exorcist,* she'll be a cliché from a family wealthy enough to ensure their children will always have a safety net. Successful casting is essential to obscure an otherwise rigid narrative formula.

Docu-dramas rely on unique and volatile characters getting tossed into a narrative frame that pressures and provokes them to irrational and spectacular reactions. *Intervention* is what some industry people call a docu-follow. The characters are chosen to fit very particular expectations to minimize radical deviations from the standard story line. The cameras "follow" along without too much interference and manipulation from the producers.

The same plotline, the same conflict, week after week, is one of the show's strengths. The ritualized narrative protects our conscience and proves, in a process more resembling the scientific method than the craft of storytelling (if we believe there is a difference), that alcoholism lies beyond the influence of policy, legislation, or social support. The coincidence of birth may have something to do with an alcoholic's chances for recovery, we are allowed to believe, but the show tells us the solution to dependency and addiction rests most firmly on the epic power of family. Experiencing the one basic plotline with superficial differences, we get our dominant cultural narratives affirmed, and those myths appear to us as protean and alive rather than scripted.

Intervention follows the suffering loved one, the antihero, filming his or her life for several weeks, to gather enough material—I'm inclined to call it "evidence"—to fill the plot points leading to the climactic moment when the antihero must choose to accept the family's terms or face exile. If the antihero accepts treatment, he wins their all-expenses-paid

trip to rehab. In my brother's case, this was a high-end facility
in Malibu. Deception is a necessary part of the deal, in that, to
justify the footage taken before the intervention, the subjects
are told that their story is contributing to a generic documentary on alcoholism and addiction. Given the popularity of the
show, any alcoholic or addict stable enough for the producers to build an episode around should also be culturally aware
enough to have heard of the show and to have its imprimatur
in mind enough to know at least the mold of the character
they've been assigned in the performance.

An intervention on *Intervention* aspires to the dramatic fris-
son of theater in the sense that theater is experienced collec-
tively: it is for us, by us, and, in the end, about us. Apart from
all else, theater is composed of a community formed to give
witness, the way a jury is to witness the production of reality
as competing interests perceive it. No matter how unreal theater may be, it is *really* happening in the presence of, and at the
behest of, the audience that judges the veracity of the performance. Theater also promises the anticipatory tension of the
actors' potential failure and humiliation.

We want something very simple from the antihero. We expect self-destruction, depravity, and an avalanche of mishaps
and bad choices. We also want his confession. We want him to
expiate our collective guilt. The family serves as a background
for calamity, a Greek chorus reciting grievances to contextual-
ize the antihero. Once the antihero's dysfunction is proven in
sufficiently gruesome testimonials and B-roll images, members
of the chorus begin to emerge in cutaway portrait interviews
as agents of his confession. If the antihero refuses treatment,
we can say, *we tried*. If the ending lacks redemption, we can
console ourselves by imagining the casket, closed, out of focus,

and accompanied by the appropriately decorous voice-over and string music. Either way, the producers get their episode, and there is no reason why they shouldn't.

The cast of the "Robby" [*sic*] episode of *Intervention* consisted of myself; my parents; my maternal grandparents, Sarah and Bob; my mom's sister, Donna; Robbie's wife, Annika; his manager—also named Bob; and Robbie's best friend, Brian. Candy, our interventionist, met with us twice. Both meetings were taped. The first meeting was intended to get us cozy with one another and familiarize us with the logistics. The second meeting reminded me of a wedding rehearsal. Candy, weathered by time and experience, exuded the beatified air of a high-ranking cleric. Her voice was worn, but comfortable and common as airport upholstery. The lines in her face indicated she had smoked cigarettes for years. Whatever commercial ambitions the producers may have had, I trusted that Candy answered to a higher moral standard. I couldn't hide anything from her. She looked at me as if we had met somewhere before, as if she could tell that I was suffering, too.

Candy asked us questions about how we felt and whether or not we were prepared to follow through with the threat to shut Robbie out of our lives if he refused to accept treatment. Some of us, like Robbie's wife, Annika, didn't answer. My mother answered yes too soon, and too confidently. Candy handed each of us a yellow legal pad, and asked us to write a letter telling Robbie how we felt his drinking had affected his life in negative ways. Everyone's first draft and most second drafts proved how much we wanted to describe the ways his drinking was fucking up *our* lives. We tended to personalize it. Who sees things from the perspective of the drunk?

In an intervention, we want the drunk to see things from

our point of view. No matter how we frame it, an intervention is retributive justice. The community takes up the burden of confession before transferring it to the antihero. The antihero doesn't need to tell his story, needn't construct a narrative of recovery, because the community will have already done this work for him. Like a sacrificial lamb, the antihero only has to step into the narrative already written, and accept responsibility for it.

Dear Rob,

I have seen your alcoholism affect your life negatively in the following ways: Your drinking makes you mistake destruction for surrender. If you want to say, "fuck it, fuck this life," you could try living without expectations. Your drinking fills you with regret, which you mistake for nostalgia, which is preferable to the emptiness of tomorrow, and more bearable, glossing over unhealed shame in search of impossible memories like so many lost love letters, as you weep at songs from the eighties. Your drinking has convinced you that frustration is Nature's transparent will, Emerson's transcendental God: the eye at the center of all consciousness. I was hoping to avoid discussing "faith," that fabric of devotions that includes love, trust, loyalty, and promises, because drunks are incapable of signing any promissory notes on their own behalf. You need skin in the game, but no ice cream scoop–sized dollop of flesh will change hands without the violence needed first to extract it. There must be pain in the bargain, which is why you have to hit rock bottom or accept this rock bottom imposed on you now by your family. You have to lose something substantial or see the

potential for catastrophic loss in terms convincing enough
to make you want to quit drinking. You have to sit with
the horror of your inability to promise, and surrender to it.
Sobriety requires the opposite of will.

My father may have pretended to, but I don't think he even
wrote one draft of the letter to Rob. Why write? Writing for
him was redundant. My father liked to paraphrase Einstein:
Insanity is doing the same thing over and over again, and expect-
ing a different outcome. But there is a reason we do the same
thing over and over again. He couldn't see that there's value in
the process and not just the outcome, which is why he couldn't
wrap his head around addiction, his own or anyone else's.

Robbie is drinking again, my mother would say. Still. Again.
She'd had it. Could take no more. I mouthed the words along
as they danced into my ear from the receiver. A child traumatized by the spectacle of her parents drunk and incoher-
ent, she gravitated toward similar exhibitions to cauterize that
unhealing wound. I hated playing along, even though I did.
My brother seemed content to ride the endless wave of her
enabling. I asked her why she didn't tell Robbie and me that
we had this family history before we developed drinking habits. She said she didn't know that people could be genetically
predisposed to alcoholism and bipolar disorder.

Jiminy Cricket or Mafia don?

Freud calls it the *repetition compulsion,* and connects this
compulsion to an infantile sexual urge, some broken con-
nection to Mom or Dad buried in the psyche. The repetition
compulsion is a closed circuit that can help us cope with addic-
tive behaviors from substance abuse to fetishistic and social

attachments. "Why didn't you tell me what I was," I asked my mother repeatedly, hoping for a different answer. "Why don't you stop rescuing Robbie if he is making your life so miserable," I asked repeatedly, knowing the answer. I'd play dumb. She'd play dumb. Shame and denial. We all pretended we didn't know what's going on. "Again, again," a toddler will say, even before the last page of the bedtime story.

Ostensibly, my mother believed that if she threatened to throw Robbie out, he would weigh his fear of losing her love against his compulsion to drink and find the scale sagging in favor of the former. She also thought that by threatening to throw Robbie out she could postpone her guilt for unconsciously enjoying his continued dependence on her and his inability to leave. We could be sure of one thing in either case. She would not throw my brother out. These were the parameters of an experiment she conducted with all of us.

Her elder son, her husband, her boyfriend(s), her younger son: we all, in finding ourselves devoted to her, committed ourselves to the laboratory of her emotional past, the nocturnal squeaking of our running wheels and the ashen light of the exit sign glinting off the bend of gooseneck faucets and beakers. Some of us were bred as subjects for these very experiments.

———

My father's maxim on insanity and repetition makes appearing normal the priority. One doesn't want to appear insane. This (among other things) prevented *me* from seeing the "repeat" I had programmed my own life to play out. The command to *do something different* kept me scrambling for set changes backstage of my waking life. While I was focused on doing things

differently, I found the details were, paradoxically, enabling. Rather than move me closer to emotional stability, "doing something different" justified my need to work the problem out anew: I fooled myself into believing it was a new problem. It came as a big fucking surprise each time I discovered that I had peed on my roommate's laundry or passed out on the hood of a parked car outside a bar. I often resolved to do "something different" like avoid brown liquor, for example, or eat at least a cheeseburger before I went out, or not drink with strangers. My resolution to drink only on every third day produced such an elaborate system of cap and trade that I confused myself into giving up the accounting. I didn't consider the possibility that I was conducting an experiment, and I didn't benefit from anything I might have learned through those repeated trials. Instead, I displaced the shame, smuggling the earliest hurt into more and deeper quarters of my subconscious to make room for fresh quotidian shames. Who could have predicted that *Intervention* would teach me this and precipitate my sobriety instead of my brother's?

———

Within two days of my mother's e-mail to A&E, the show's producers had her on a conference call. They deputized her as casting agent, and made arrangements through her to interview the relevant friends and family. Naturally, they needed me to participate.

Dear Rob,
    I must have ridden the Q train in a blackout all night, shuttling between Coney Island and 63rd St. Like a

diving bell resurfacing, I came to sitting on a retaining
wall facing the Plaza Hotel. My cell phone was dead. My
jacket and messenger bag, containing my laptop, wallet,
and notebooks, were missing. If I had been mugged it was
peaceful because I didn't feel any aches or bruises on my
body. The Apple Store, its glass cube behind me, had just
opened for the day. Pretending to shop, I loitered while
charging my phone. I promised myself I would never
drink again. Ginger had to pack up the girls and drive
into Manhattan to pick me up on what should have been
a leisurely Saturday morning of bagels and coffee. That
afternoon, someone from the MTA called the house. A
good Samaritan turned in my bag, and told the subway
ticket agent that I walked off the train and left everything
behind when I reached my stop. But it was a random
stop, Bryant Park. Why would I get off the train at Bryant
Park? What was I walking away from? And how could I
have then walked nearly twenty blocks to 59th Street in a
blackout? It was a miracle that the person who witnessed
my attempted life-escape was kind enough to deliver my
things to the ticket office for safekeeping. A miracle is a
happy occasion, right? Good fortune. The laws of nature
suspended. I took the subway back into Manhattan to pick
up my stuff and decided it was time to celebrate. I went
out drinking again. I had so many chances to recognize
the mess I made of my life, and I kept ignoring them. We
are giving you a gift today like that stranger on the train
gave me a gift. We are giving you a reason to stop drinking
before you do any mortal harm. We are offering to help
you get your life back. This is a miracle. Put down the
drink and walk away. I wish it were that easy.

When my mother called me to share the news and to complain about Robbie, I was two hundred miles from home, in my new office at the university where I had started teaching only a few weeks earlier. Ginger had decided not to participate in this leg of my career development, and refused to leave New York. Years later, she explained that my drinking had surpassed the regularly disturbing levels she was accustomed to, and that she could not move to a new city where she would be alone to contend with my random disappearances. She'd rather I was gone altogether. Instead, I commuted, spending half the week away from home. After I gave Ginger my paycheck, all I could afford was a rented room, which I found in the home of another writer. My older daughter, Sara, had just started kindergarten, and Fita was still an infant. Each week I came home to find the girls had achieved some milestone in my absence. The emotional cost of missing out on my family life was steep. I had convinced myself the job was worth it. When my conviction wavered, from the start, I used alcohol and the petty dramas I concocted while drunk to distract myself. I was hungover when my mother called.

At first, she played Jiminy Cricket. Instead of asking me to be on the show, my mother asked if I would support the intervention to get Robbie into a Malibu rehab that cost more per month than I made in a year. I knew the college professor big brother would make a great foil for the rock star baby brother. But I couldn't play the role. In proximity to my brother's stellar implosion, I was afraid I might blurt out, compulsively confessional, that I, too, was a train wreck. I was afraid that the world would finally know (as if it didn't already) my secret. I was a drunk. My new colleagues at my new job would spurn me. My friends would distance themselves from me. I was too fragile to withstand humiliation. "Can't do it," I told my mother, but she appealed. I declined again, and she sighed, assuring me all I had to do was talk to the producers so they could get a better understanding of Robbie's path to perdition. "All I'm asking," she said, "is that you at least speak to the people. Just talk to them." I knew that if I made the smallest concession, I would find myself surrounded by an array of lighting umbrellas, boom mics, and soft boxes.

The project threatened my mental and emotional health. They were asking me to appear without pretense, affect, or authority. I did not care to see myself as a supporting character. To my mind, they were asking me to reveal an unguarded version of myself that I'd worked for years to repress. My ego in league with my vanity, my subconscious started telling me to offer them instead a plot twist, a competing antihero poised to claim the spotlight.

"This isn't about you," my mother said. She promised I wouldn't have to appear on the show. All she wanted was to get my part of the story for context. But, much as my private self wanted to run to an idling Town Car with a jacket over my head, ducking the paparazzi, my public self still wanted everyone to know that I was at the center of attention.

I decided I could make the producers regret having bet on the wrong pony. I agreed to a phone interview, knowing full well I would appear on the show.

A woman named Katie called. Katie and I spoke for three fucking hours. Until then, I considered myself a consummate listener. I hadn't yet seen a therapist, and this was the first time a person without a stake in either my well-being or my humiliation had asked me, with sincere interest—who cares what motivated that interest—to share. Katie explained to me the show sought to capture the "Come to Jesus moment," as she called it. I imagined myself as twelve-year-old Langston Hughes sitting on the mourner's bench among a lineup of little sinners. In his autobiography *The Big Sea*, Hughes describes his Come to Jesus moment as a flop, a moment of non-salvation. His devout aunt prepared him for an event culminating after a weeks-long revival at her church. All the children participated. That day, every child except Hughes walked up to the altar and into the preacher's embrace. Christ entered their hearts. They were saved. It was a kiddie pageant of religious fervor. Hughes waited to feel what his aunt had described to him as a kind of acid trip of salvation. When, finally, he was the last child sitting, proof he hadn't experienced the psychedelic light, his aunt knelt by him and wept for his obstinacy. The congregation prayed and sang for him alone. The minister's entreaties grew more pointed. Although he hadn't experienced Christ entering his heart, out of frustration and embarrassment and for the sake of expediency, little Hughes stood and shuffled to the altar. He believed he was a fraud, a sinner in lamb's clothing welcomed into the fold. "I had lied," writes Hughes. "I had deceived everybody in the church." And, because of this deception, he could no longer believe in Jesus. But Hughes's sacrifice was not in vain. The congregation's needs were fulfilled.

I revealed to Katie my deeply held convictions: offhand analyses of my brother and his upbringing compared with mine; how I thought my mother prevented Robbie from completing what he started and how this caused him to disrespect the achievements he had; my fear that Robbie wouldn't be able to live without the emotional support of a woman; my guilt at having been such a shitty, unsupportive brother. All these I offered up for my interviewer's delectation. She had the patience of a claims adjuster. She had earned my trust, and I wanted to reward her.

I said her name frequently, as if I was flirting. I was flirting. I had a sports water bottle on my desk that I was sipping from because I was dehydrated from the night before. "I didn't know what an alcoholic was, Katie," I droned, "but even when I was eighteen, I knew I would have to stop drinking one day. I thought somehow it would happen on its own, that I would reach 'the end' naturally. That I wouldn't have to do anything more than wait it out. You know, Katie, there was a water tower in my hometown that I used to imagine held an undisclosed quantity of booze. I imagined I was assigned that mysterious amount of booze at birth, and that I *had* to drink it. I had to keep drinking, faithfully, until the water tower gurgled like an empty milkshake. I could try to drink it as fast as I could, and be done with it while I was still young, but that strategy, if it didn't kill me before I drained the tower, could cause so much physical damage I wouldn't be able to enjoy what life I had left. If I took my time with it, on the other hand, set the pump for a slow and constant drip, I'd be traumatized like a torture victim, and unable to respond appropriately to or interpret everyday experiences. I have felt helpless each day, my fingers crossed that the nightmare would soon end. And I'd hope I wasn't run over or thrown in jail or that I wouldn't hurt anyone before I could enjoy life again." I purged. I cleansed my soul, and felt transformed. I promised my eventual recovery (but not yet), and I wanted more of what Katie was dealing. For her, I agreed to be on the show.

Being away from my family each week was demoralizing. I'd get on the bus in New York, and four hours later I was in a city where no one knew me or my habits. I had no social network to keep me stable or give me a sense of who I was. I could be anybody or nobody. I cultivated a community the best way I knew how, at a bar, until I could no longer square the doting, involved father I wanted to be with the drunken poetry professor I had become. One Sunday morning, I woke up early on my office floor, having shit my pants. There was no one in the halls. The building was empty. I washed my underwear in the men's room sink. The figure in the mirror frightened me, and I chastised myself for being such a caricature. One of those self-help sayings suddenly came to mind: take care of your body as if it belonged to someone you love.

When Ginger was finally pregnant with our first child, I panicked. No matter that we were married and had expressed to ourselves and others our desire to have children, Ginger's pregnancy seemed a symptom of social ill and proof of our impending class stagnation. I also panicked because I thought I had stolen Ginger's future. I couldn't trust myself to sacrifice part of my future as co-parenting would require.

Parenthood seemed so abstract that I reacted to it with academic interest. I think Ginger reacted similarly. We treated her pregnancy like a standardized test. Like our score would be on our permanent record, which it would. We took Lamaze classes. When Ginger's water broke, it was like we had just been given the command to pick up our pencils and begin. I felt awkward and useless at the birth, so I took pictures to memorialize our accomplishment. As the baby's head was cresting, I wrenched the lens of my SLR camera this way and that. I focused on the field of depth rather than the miracle of life. Then the nurse suctioned some goop out of the baby's mouth and it screamed for the first time, and I was shocked to imagine that the tiny animal the nurse had placed on Ginger's chest would one day ask to borrow my car.

Sara was perfect. I mean, she was flawless like an experiment in eugenics. Fita was born with a hole in her heart and a birthmark that crawled along her jawline to her ear. I have a similar birthmark on my chest, and the coincidence suggested an omen of some sort, though I was afraid to interpret it. I sat beside the plastic NICU box that held her, and wept and prayed. I prayed sincerely for the second time in my adult life. My imagination ran wild with fear. In time, the hole closed, and Fita grew up healthy. Whenever I walked with Fita in the baby harness on my chest, I'd watch as people on the street were struck dumb, mesmerized by my child's beauty. My children felt magical and empowering. I had been chosen to protect them, as I was chosen to protect my brother. Living alone in a rented room in a city far from my family, I was failing my responsibility.

Because it is eternal, alcoholism is the closest thing I have to religion. Relapse can leap from the pantry in a bottle of vanilla extract or ambush from a crowded picnic table where a red plastic Solo cup of chardonnay sits beside a cup of ginger ale. There can be no happily ever after for a recovering drunk like me. Relapse could hide in the promise of anonymity I might find in the looks strangers give me on the streets of a foreign city. *Have a drink,* they say, *you are not accountable to us.* Relapse can seduce me with the confidence that I've "got my drinking under control" or that I'm "getting better."

The threat never dies, and yet every alcoholic has a bottom.

Each bottom is a unique point of depravity determined in the balance of self-esteem, personal will, and the need to be emotionally connected to others. For so many, alcoholism is the public face of other pathologies. For every drunk lucky enough to struggle with the habit of drink alone, there are countless more plunging through the false bottoms of undiagnosed mental illness.

"What do you want to listen to?" asked the cameraman. He was a solid decade younger than me, and still had a college-boy mien. "Name an artist." His laptop was open, two fingers scrolling.

"What do you have?" I asked.

"What are you feeling like?" He wanted to lighten my mood, which was salty from the argument with my father, and he may also have felt guilty for chasing us down the hall to record the fracas.

In addition to a hotel room upstairs that they used for the one-on-ones, the crew had booked a medium-sized conference room for the big event. Toward the back, farthest from the door, they'd arranged two sofas and two club chairs in an L-shape. On the right was the head-of-household chair reserved for Candy. The chair for the guest of honor radiated with the spectral presence of Rob's future. The Baby New Year of his rebirth, like Schrödinger's cat, both sober and drunk at once, the accumulated projections of all our hopes, guarded optimism, and cynical fears. There was a plastic plant in the corner. Off to the side of the room, safely out of view of the cameras, was the catering table.

My father and I had gotten into an argument over the cold

cuts. My patience with him was thinning, and the slightest static between us flared into full-blown electrical storms. "You see the place they're sending him to," he had asked. "Malibu, cliff side. High-class stuff."

"Oh my god, Dad, it's a fucking rehab, not a resort!"

"Well, if you gotta go, may as well be in style," he said.

"Seriously, this is why we're even here in the first place. You people are so caught up in the image, you can't deal with the reality." As I spoke, I noticed the cameraman had quietly trained the camera on us from the periphery. My dad was dismissive as usual at first, but he quickly turned defensive.

"What would you have done? Turn him out into the street?"

"You've never given him a chance to rely on his own resources. So yes, maybe you should have turned him out into the street," I said. The camera got closer and more conspicuous. "You didn't have a problem putting me out of the house."

"Grow up. That's not what happened, and you know it," my father said. "You cut out." He noticed the camera, and started walking toward the door. "You cut yourself out of the picture. That's what you do." I followed him. The camera followed behind me.

"This from a man who abandons his grandchildren for a fantasy life in Vegas?"

By now he was speed walking down the corridor outside the conference room. We could hear the cameraman, who had been joined by another crew member, and their equipment made a racket as they jogged to keep up.

"Grandchildren!" he shouted. "*Sara* was mine for a while until you put her in that school," he said. His breathing was labored, and it reminded me that he was still very sick. He stopped to rest, and leaned against a pillar near the wall. "And

I've already lost Fita." He had his back to me, wedged between the pillar and the wall.

"Already lost? This is how you think? Deciding who is with you and who's against? You think only people completely devoted to you can love you?" The camera's light was now in my face, and I noticed myself performing for it. *I was stealing the show!* "Wait, are you *hiding* from the camera?" I demanded.

He whispered something, but it wasn't out of shame or embarrassment. He didn't want to be seen out of character. I told him to speak up, knowing this would make great television, but he whispered again. "I'd rather have him sick and with me than to be alone."

———

Someone was getting texts to update us. "They're leaving the house." Then, "They're ten minutes away." Candy told us all to take our places as we had rehearsed earlier in the day. It felt like a surprise party. Robbie arrived carrying a water bottle. When he confirmed that this was what he thought it was, he stopped in the middle of the conference room and began chugging the water bottle. "I guess that's not water," Annika said.

Robbie approached the imaginary altar baptizing himself with vodka. My lamb, my baby brother, was coming for absolution. No one else in the room, I'd decided, was prepared or qualified to receive him as I was. Much as she cared, Candy wasn't, and could not be, emotionally invested. My father had no moral standing. My mother kept her clinical distance. I alone would lift Robbie's burden from him, and carry it myself. "Will you accept this gift of treatment that we are offering you today?" I held my open arms, willing him into my embrace.

———

Years later, we had all settled back into a kind of détente. Robbie was drinking publicly again. He was "doing much better," but in cycles. My mother had stopped complaining about him—to me, at least. My father was dead. Producers from the show were planning a "where are they now" episode, and called to find out how Robbie's sobriety was going. If there was ever a chance to prove that he was rehabilitated, and get back into the industry, this was it. But no one had the energy for the charade.

It had been maybe five months since our father died when Robbie went into the hospital. I got around to calling him, as my mother had encouraged me to do. As if his injury was a broken vase in the living room explained away as an innocent fluke of physics. Robbie insisted that his record intake did not incite the mania with which he'd so recently filed down the corn on his foot, attacking it as if that barnacle were the distillation of all his spiritual suffering. Alcohol was not responsible, he claimed, for distracting him from the pain of the wound that he happened to discover in the place where the corn had so recently been. Alcohol did not thin his blood to make way for the infection that swelled his ankle and occasioned a call on the local emergency ward. His drinking had nothing to do, said he, with the fact that he'd allowed his health insurance to lapse or that he'd missed so many days of work that his job would be reluctant to grant him disability pay, giving him reason to delay that call on the emergency ward. It was not a crisis, but merely a "setback," that he had to have an ice cream scoop–sized chunk of his infected calf removed and grafted over with skin from his ass cheek.

These setbacks were familiar. He'd had them before the intervention, and he would have them again. I was still a shitty big brother, mostly observing Rob from afar. As with his childhood manias, Robbie's alcoholism was a bellwether for my own. In him, I saw my life foreshadowed in double time, a fun-house mirror, a pratfalling, slapstick ghost of Christmas Future. The upside of my side-eye surveillance was that I became an expert diagnostician of Robbie's pathologies. I knew that, like the Old Lady who swallowed a fly and then had to consume incrementally larger beasts to conquer the escalating shame of that original lapse in judgment, Robbie was drinking in search of a cure.

Robbie told me about a younger coworker in the warehouse where he worked who was starstruck by him, and told Robbie every day that he was going to make it in the music business just like Robbie did. "Young bucks see me, and they think it's easy. But you gotta have talent. I try to tell them it's not about the glamour. Kids don't want to listen."

I wanted to ask him before I let him off the phone: "What did you see as my role in the family?"

"You were the reason I thought it was okay to drink," he said, chuckling. "You were always fucking up. Mommy and Daddy kept saying—everybody knew how smart you were, but it was a blessing and a curse. I thought that was just how we were supposed to be," he said with a shrug in his voice. The tragic artist. Passionate, disturbed, angsty. "What's the term?" he asked rhetorically. *Artist manqué?* I thought. *Poète maudit? Finicky aesthete? Bohemian raconteur?* "Idiot savant," he said. "Yeah, you were some kind of idiot savant." This was exactly how I thought of *him*. The thing we're critical of in others is often the thing we fear is most true of ourselves. The timeless wisdom of the playground endures: "it takes one to know one."

While I was studying the lessons of Robbie's destructive path, I may have been influencing my subject, drawing him into my orbit. In studying my family's destruction, I am studying my own.

Of course, I should have "been there" for him. Of course, I should have fought for him. He's my fucking brother. When he was starting, I was a veteran drunk. Could some part of me have wished my demons onto Robbie back then? The old fears and insecurities are still with me, robust as ever. And I still know, like Robbie, what it feels like to be trapped in my head with a toxic imagination. It takes one to know one.

And like that it caught up with me like a dimly remembered arrest warrant from a distant state: the past. When friends tell me stories from the bad old days, I'd shake my head no: "It wasn't me" or "I don't remember nothing." I lived like an ice cube in a deep-fryer. Back then, I kept the music loud. But my brother dragged it up through the fog, and here it is, my past, shaking its booty in front of me, calling me out. What I used to do to harm myself—scares the shit out of me to remember. *In the desert of Itabira things come back to life,* the Brazilian poet Carlos Drummond de Andrade writes. Memory. Like pulling the chain on the ceiling light and bringing the plaster down on my head.

In the extended version of *Intervention* available online, there is a coda that the original broadcast left out. It shows Rob at the rehab in Malibu near the end of his treatment. You can tell he's been sober; his eyes are clear. His speech is crisp.

You can trace the edges of his thoughts. He's explaining to a counselor-doctor-whatever that his big brother has published a book of poetry. He's showing off a copy of my first book, showing off the dedication page where it reads, "for Robby." God, I didn't even spell his name right. In the video, he marvels at the book, proud of me. "What an honor," he says, like I did him a favor.

Acknowledgments

I'd like to thank Aunt Cynthia, who knows all the Pardlo business; Aunt Donna, for permission to decorate her story in "Minority Business Consortium," which she originally relayed unembellished like pages of a coloring book; Aunt Robin, my first best friend in life.

Along with my friend and mentor Phillip Lopate, I am indebted to Leslie Jamison, Melissa Febos, Vievee Francis, Colin Channer, Kwame Dawes, Ira Silverberg and Bob Morris, Tayari Jones, Nick Flynn, Maaza Mengiste, Ravi Howard, and, as always, The Moxie Family.

Heartfelt gratitude to the many teachers who invested time and energy in me only because it was in them to do.

For the sake of public appearances, I also have to thank Ginger, the true drill instructor of my life. I wouldn't otherwise presume any words of thanks could suffice.

A NOTE ON THE TYPE

The text of this book was set in Sabon, a typeface designed by Jan Tschichold (1902–1974), the well-known German typographer. Based loosely on the original designs by Claude Garamond (ca. 1480–1561), Sabon is unique in that it was explicitly designed for hot-metal composition on both the Monotype and Linotype machines as well as for filmsetting. Designed in 1966 in Frankfurt, Sabon was named for the famous Lyons punch cutter Jacques Sabon, who is thought to have brought some of Garamond's matrices to Frankfurt.

Typeset by Scribe,
Philadelphia, Pennsylvania

Printed and bound by Berryville Graphics,
Berryville, Virginia

Designed by Cassandra J. Pappas